2
245

Black American Literature
Essays

A CHARLES E. MERRILL LITERARY TEXT

CHARLES E. MERRILL LITERARY TEXTS

Under the General Editorship of
Matthew J. Bruccoli and Joseph Katz

Anthologies by genre, period, theme, or other significant principle for the study of American literature. Each volume provides reliable texts introduced by a noted authority.

Textual Note

This volume presents authoritative texts for all material. The selections are reprinted from their original appearances as specified in each case.

Black American Literature
Essays

Edited by

Darwin T. Turner

Professor of English & Dean
of the Graduate School
North Carolina Agricultural and
Technical State University

Charles E. Merrill Publishing Company
A Bell & Howell Company
Columbus, Ohio

Standard Book Number: 675-09503-4

Library of Congress Catalog Number: 70-76451

2   3   4   5   6   7   8   9   10   11   12 — 76   75   74   73   72   71   70   69

Printed in the United States of America

To my grandmother,
Who was proud,
and
To Mother and Dad,
Who are.

Preface

A word, perhaps, needs to be said about the title. When James Baldwin wrote, "Nobody knows my name," he could not have foreseen the violent dispute which would be incited a decade later by those who, rejecting the term "Negro," wish to be described as "black." The title of this volume indicates my awareness of and sympathy with that group even if I cannot totally agree with their argument.

The controversy is not trivial. It reflects a troubled, sometimes desperate search for identity by a people who have lived in a society which consciously stripped their racial identity from them. Originally, we were African, but we were taken from Africa. Voluntarily or involuntarily, we mixed with people of other nations and other races; but, as long as our skin remained dark and our features Negroid, we were identified as Negroes rather than as members of any other ethnic or political group. And, despite our three-century existence in America, we have never been recognized fully as Americans. Because of such a history, we have sought to retain or regain our identity and to proclaim that identity with a meaningful name.

Early in the twentieth century, the term "colored" linked the causes of the black American with other dark-skinned peoples of the world. To others, "Afro-American" seemed a more accurate description of our identity. Then, a solution seemed to lie in a crusade to capitalize "negro" and thus change it from a sometimes derogatory description to the name of a racially proud group. Now, rejecting "Negro" as a term which they identify with slavery and servility, many members of the group insist upon "black."

In this work I shall use "black" generally to contrast with "white" and most often to identify individuals of African ancestry who wrote in this country before the United States gained its identity as a nation. I shall also use "black" specifically to refer to writers identified with Black Nationalism or with the Black Arts Movement. Frequently, however, I shall use "black," "Afro-American," and "Negro" interchangeably. My reason — if I need one — is not that I am too old to change my habits but that I have struggled too diligently to discover my own identity to permit it to be dislodged by the mere question of whether I am called "Negro" or "black."

Let me take this opportunity to express a very deep appreciation to Mrs. Fannie Garrison and Mrs. Nina Bridges, who helped type this work, and to Miss Myrtle Howard, whose general assistance was invaluable. I wish also to express gratitude to my wife, Jeanne, who endured while I wrote.

CONTENTS

Black American Literature
Essays

Introduction

Unlike the essayists most frequently studied in literature courses, black essayists were created by need rather than by desire. White Joseph Addison and Richard Steele established *The Tatler* and *The Spectator* periodicals to provide a medium for their polished, witty comments about the manners, morals, customs, and activities of eighteenth-century Londoners. In 1827, black David Russwurm published the first issue of *Freedom's Journal* to voice black men's cries for liberation. In nineteenth-century England, white Charles Lamb and Robert Louis Stevenson momentarily escaped from thoughts of personal troubles by writing charming, humorous, or sentimental essays. In 1829, black David Walker in a pamphlet, *Appeal,* urged slaves to rebel.

There are obvious reasons for the more utilitarian motives of black writers. First, because literate black men were scarce, most who could write effectively assumed — or were forced to assume — the responsibility of speaking for Negroes, individually or as a group. Second, publishers — whether nineteenth-century Abolitionists or twentieth-century editors — most often have been interested in publicizing the words of a black writer if he addressed himself to "The Negro Problem." Through the centuries, the specific issues have varied: protests against slavery; biographical or historical presentations of the cultural achievements of black men; protests against lynching; arguments about education, job opportunities, voting rights, legal rights, civil rights, housing. Despite the seeming variety, always there is "The Cause," developed in two dominant themes — (1) protests against unjust treatment of Negroes and (2) defenses of Negroes based on their contributions to America.

Because of this sustained emphasis upon purpose, the short nonfiction writings of black Americans have been judged more frequently according to the popular appeal of the subject-matter

1

rather than the literary skill of the writer. Nevertheless, during the nineteenth century, and increasingly during the twentieth, black writers have demonstrated rhetorical skill in short, nonfiction works. This slim volume offers a collection of works from some of the best-known and most talented Afro-American essayists of those two centuries.

"Essay," of course, is a vague term, which may describe many different forms of writing. Here, it is restricted to any short, nonfiction development of a single theme. As such, it includes pamphlets and letters, which, in the eighteenth and nineteenth centuries, were a popular form of literature. In the sense in which it is used, however, "essay" does not include speeches, designed for oral rather than written presentation. Nor does it include sections of longer works, such as histories and biographies, unless those longer works are merely collections of disparate essays rather than unified compositions. These criteria, therefore, exclude the works of some individuals who have been important as orators, historians, political leaders, religious leaders, intellectual leaders, poets, novelists, or dramatists, but who have not earned reputations for artistic excellence as essayists.

Such a collection serves four main purposes. First, by furnishing samples of the styles of the best-known black essayists, it affords a comparison of their work with that of their more frequently anthologized white contemporaries. Second, it provides opportunity for examination of the changes in style from the nineteenth to the twentieth century. Third, the personal and cultural essays offer glimpses into the thoughts of individual men about subjects other than the social, economic, and political struggles of Negroes. In all of these, this collection reflects, in miniature, the history of essay writing by black Americans.

The earliest essay known to have been published is *Address to Negroes in the State of New York* (1787), a pamphlet by Jupiter Hammon, who twenty-seven years earlier had become the first black American to publish a poem. Undistinguished in style or thought, Hammon's address urged Negroes to conduct themselves well.

This admonitory tone did not set a pattern for the essays which followed in pre-Civil War America. As has been stated earlier, most either protested against unjust treatment of Negroes or defended Negroes, primarily by pointing out their achievements and contributions.

One style of defense is apparent in *A Narrative of the Proceedings of the Black People during the Late Awful Calamity in*

Philadelphia; and a Refutation of Some Censures Thrown upon Them in Some Late Publications (1794). This pamphlet, written by Absalom Jones and Richard Allen, organizers of the Free African Society, praised Negroes for helping during an epidemic of yellow fever. In a similar vein are pamphlets by James Forten and Russell Parrott (1818), by Lydia Child (1833), and by Robert Purvis (1838). All call attention to unjust treatment of Negroes.

Another style of defense is typified by William Wells Brown's *The Black Man: His Antecedents, His Genius and His Achievements* (1863), which was expanded into *The Rising Son* (1874). Each work is a collection of essays praising the achievements of both famous and almost unknown individuals of African descent.

Most essayists writing prior to the Civil War preferred to attack slavery rather than to defend Negroes. Possibly the earliest, certainly the best-known of these, was David Walker, author of *Appeal*, an incendiary treatise urging slaves to rebel. Equally bold, if less well-known, were David Ruggles, who defended the New York Anti-Slavery Society by attacking its attackers, and Reverend Hosea Eaton, who, tracing the cultural heritage of black men, sought to prove the inferiority of white men.

Many of the attacks on slavery appeared in newspapers and periodicals edited by Negroes. The earliest of these, *Freedom's Journal* (1827), was edited by Samuel E. Cornish, a minister, and John B. Russwurm, the first black man to graduate from a college in the United States. It was followed in 1829 by *Rights for All*, edited by Cornish, and by *The Colored American* (1837–41), which included among its several editors Cornish and James McCune Smith, a graduate of the University of Glasgow, who is described by the editors of *The Negro Caravan* as "the most learned Negro of the antebellum period." Of the 100 newspapers which Smith estimated that Negroes attempted prior to 1855, the best-known and most enduring was Frederick Douglass's *The North Star*, published as a weekly from 1847 to 1860.

Not all black writers were polarized to attack or defense. In 1831, Maria W. Stewart published her first collection of devotional essays, *Religion and the Pure Principles of Morality*. In 1851 and again in 1855, William C. Nell published biographical sketches of Negroes who had served in the armed forces. In 1852, Martin R. Delany, a physician, scientist, novelist, and political writer, wrote *The Condition, Elevation, Emigration, and Destiny of the Colored People of the United States, Politically Considered*. Like Hammon before him, Delany concerned himself more with the question of what Negroes could do to improve themselves than with the problem of what was being done to them. In the same year, William Wells Brown, who wrote the first novel and the first drama by a black American, published a collection of letters, *Three Years in Europe; or, Places I Have Seen and People I Have Met.* Brown concentrated on lyric or entertaining descriptions of his observations and activities, but he never fully escaped awareness of the problems of enslaved Americans. In 1862, Alexander Crummell, one of the most learned men of his time, published *The Future of Africa,* a collection of essays and sermons objectively examining the future possibilities for Africans.

The patterns established prior to the Civil War also characterized essay writing by Negroes in the last half of the nineteenth century. For example, although he had supposed that Emancipation would relieve him from the need to continue to champion the Negro cause, Frederick Douglass kept his pen busy during Reconstruction, first joining with others to urge the passage of a Civil Rights bill, then participating in the protests against the Supreme Court decision which declared the bill unconstitutional.

Two issues in particular stimulated the interest of black essayists during the last decade of the nineteenth century and the first decade of the twentieth. One was the Booker T. Washington–W. E. B. DuBois controversy. In 1895, at the Atlanta Exposition, one of the featured speakers was Booker T. Washington, founder of Tuskegee Institute. While urging whites to grant additional economic opportunities to blacks, Washington promised that Negroes would renounce their interests in social or political equality. In addition, he stressed the need for industrial education to a degree which seemed to minimize the desirability of any other kind of education for Negroes. W. E. B. DuBois, who led the objections to Washington's conciliatory policy, was joined by such writers as Kelly Miller, a professor at Howard University, and William Monroe Trotter, a Boston journalist.

The second issue was the abusive treatment of Negroes at the end of the century. Finding sufficient support in Booker T. Washington's endorsement of social separation, Southern legislators passed laws to enforce segregation and to deprive Negroes of all political rights. And the North acquiesced. The federal government could not defend the equality of American Negroes when, to justify its foreign policy in Latin America and the Philippines, it implied that all dark-skinned people are inferior creatures who need masters. The intensified discrimination and increasing acts of violence produced such collections of essays as *The Negro Problem* (1903), to which Chesnutt, Dunbar, Washington, and DuBois contributed, and *How to Solve the Race Problem* (1904).

Despite the continuing emphasis on racial problems, three significant changes are evident in essays written between 1900 and 1960. First, improving educational opportunities so expanded the number of competent essayists that no brief history can include all of the works and writers who might be mentioned. Second, particularly after 1920, the tone of essays shifted from defense to presentation. That is, no longer feeling inferior, Negro essayists sensed no compulsion to disprove their inferiority. Instead, they concentrated on explaining their needs and their desires. Third, as pride and confidence have developed among Negro writers and other intellectuals, there has been a diminution of the tendency to overpraise members of the race. Exaltation has been replaced by critical evaluation.

The most significant collections of essays written between 1900 and 1940 are W. E. B. DuBois's *The Souls of Black Folk* (1903) and Alain Locke's *The New Negro* (1925). Both are important interpretations of the character and spirit of Negroes. DuBois's work, which is evidenced later in this book, is, despite its age, an extremely perceptive presentation of the nature and sentiments and aspirations of black people, particularly those who live in the South. *The New Negro* interprets a different group — the young Negro writers and artists who clustered in Harlem during the 1920's.

Inspired by the enthusiasm and the idealism which pervaded America in the decade following World War I, numbers of talented artists earned their first national fame. "King" Oliver, Louis Armstrong, and Duke Ellington organized their orchestras. Several Negro writers and performers collaborated on *Shuffle Along* (1921), a musical comedy, which became so popular that it was moved from Harlem to Broadway — the first time that a Broadway theatre had ever presented a musical written, produced, and performed by Negroes. Florence Mills and Josephine Baker appeared professionally for the first time.

Literary artists also flourished. Claude McKay, Jean Toomer, Jessie Fauset, Countee Cullen, Langston Hughes, Wallace Thurman, Zora Neale Hurston, and Arna Bontemps published their first significant works. James Weldon Johnson edited the first anthology of poetry by Negroes, *The Book of American Negro Poetry* (1922). Within the decade, Cullen edited a second, and

Locke co-edited a collection of plays about Negro life. *The Crisis* and *Opportunity* magazines encouraged and published young black writers. Benjamin Brawley continued to publicize the achievements of Negroes, and Carter G. Woodson finished the first edition of *The Negro in Our History*. In the midst of this exciting decade, Locke, a professor of philosophy at Howard University, published his record of the achievements and his interpretation of the spirit of the "new" Negro.

Everyone, it seems, was writing essays during the Twenties. Negro periodicals needed writers: Jessie Fauset and Dorothy West, novelists of the Thirties, and Countee Cullen, a talented poet, were contributing editors. Negro newspapers needed writers. *The Baltimore Afro-American, The Chicago Defender, The Atlanta Daily World, The Pittsburgh Courier* were merely a few which offered space to young writers such as the satirical, outspoken George Schuyler, who became associate editor of *The Courier*. One-man newspapers flourished. An excellent example is Wendell P. Dabney's *The Union*, published in Cincinnati, Ohio. Magazines edited by whites sought black writers. They did not seek to hide the racial identities as earlier editors had concealed those of Charles Chesnutt and James Weldon Johnson. Instead, they advertised the racial heritage of such a talented writer as Langston Hughes. All these offered opportunity to the brash young Negroes, who, exuding confidence and pride, irreverently laughed at the old idols and ideals.

The Thirties and Forties were dominated by academic and political essayists. Such academicians as Sterling Brown and E. Franklin Frazier of Howard were evaluating the literary and social conditions of Negroes. Brown, in fact, succeeded Brawley as the major literary historian for Negroes. *Phylon* (Atlanta University), *The Journal of Negro Education*, and *The Journal of Negro History* were only a few of the scholarly journals established to give voice to the black academic community. Like many other intellectuals during the Depression, several Negro writers temporarily espoused Communism: Richard Wright, W. E. B. DuBois, and Langston Hughes were among these. Excellent histories, biographies, and other books of nonfiction abound, and individual essays are excellent. But in the twenty-year period, no significant collection of essays was produced. Perhaps the most famous individual essay is "The Ethics of Living Jim Crow" (1937), Richard Wright's recollections of incidents which taught him the behavior which is expected from a Southern Negro.

The past two decades have produced a spate of talented essayists and brilliant essays at a time at which critical issues have
required spokesmen. At the beginning of the period is Saunders Redding's *On Being Negro in America* (1951), a collection of personal
essays in which he defines and describes the black experience. The
political leaders have communicated with the vast audience which
reads newspapers and periodicals. Roy Wilkins, executive secretary of the National Association for the Advancement of
Colored People, writes editorials published regularly in Negro
newspapers, but these editorials generally are valued more for
their ideas than for their style. Civil rights leaders, such as
James Farmer, formerly head of the Congress on Racial Equality
(CORE), and Stokely Carmichael, formerly head of the Student
Non-violent Coordinating Committee (SNCC), have written articles, but their remarkable talents are best demonstrated in their
speeches. Even more, Malcolm X, a brilliant leader, was an orator
rather than a writer. The exception was Martin Luther King, Jr. An
eloquent and moving speaker — as a minister should be, he was also
a polished writer. "Letter from a Birmingham Jail," in particular,
is a model of rhetoric.

Professional writers also have revitalized the essay to explain
their reactions to critical issues. In *White Man, Listen!* (1964),
Richard Wright examined the culture and aspirations of black
people. Calvin Hernton, in *White Papers for White Americans*
(1967), has interpreted current inter-racial issues and has ana-
lyzed the artistic and racial stances of Sidney Poitier and James
Baldwin. Poet LeRoi Jones has set forth thoughts on various
subjects in *Home: Social Essays* (1966). In *Shadow and Act*
(1966) Ralph Ellison published a collection of intelligent, philosophical comments about literature and music. The most gifted
professional writer and essayist, however, is James Baldwin who,
more effectively than any writer since DuBois, has expressed
the meaning of existence as a black man in America.

Since 1960, the work of the younger black writers has been
characterized by a new awareness of the Black identity. Like the
New Negro Movement of the Twenties and the Negro Revolution
of the Fifties, the present Black Revolution is an effort by black
Americans to clarify their identity and to determine the appropriate bases for the pride and dignity essential to the moral survival
of human beings. The significant difference is that, for the first
time in America, black intellectuals do not merely admit cultural
differences which distinguish them from white countrymen; in-

stead, they reject the cultural standards evolved for the white community. The distinction is sometimes subtle but significant. Young blacks do not defend the achievements of black Americans in the manner of William Wells Brown. They do not exaggerate their differences as exotic qualities in the manner of essayists of the Renaissance. Unlike Redding and Martin Luther King, they do not solicit understanding and compassion for black Americans. They even seem to reject James Baldwin's habit of criticizing Americans with the hope of reforming them. Instead, they tell Americans what is wrong with Americans, and they use individualized vocabularies and styles rather than those approved by literary tradition. This is the style of LeRoi Jones, after 1960, and of Eldridge Cleaver.

From Hammon's labored admonition to Cleaver's throbbing condemnation is less than two hundred years in time but more than two hundred light years in thought. Black essayists came of age, then rejected the age.

Like the turbulent years of the Civil War and Reconstruction, the times seem to call for men who can articulate the issues of the day, and the men are here. Each year seems to bring more essayists into view. It is not surprising. Articulate black writers exist. They are hidden only from a literary public which is hostile or indifferent to their existence. Their ideas have meaning for American readers; and, as this book illustrates, their styles can be rhetorical models in a study of the art of the essay.

William Wells Brown (1816-1884)

Letter XI

Born a slave in Lexington, Kentucky, William Wells Brown became the most productive, versatile, and popular Negro writer of his generation. When he was nineteen, he escaped from slavery, took the name "Wells Brown" in honor of a Quaker who had befriended him, and turned his attention to ways to help those who were still enslaved. As a steward on a Lake Erie steamer, he arranged for many fugitives to flee to Canada. In 1844, he became an agent of the Western New York Anti-Slavery Society and later replaced Frederick Douglass with the Massachusetts Anti-Slavery Society. Sent to Europe as a delegate to the Paris Peace Conference, he remained for several years because of the harsh fugitive slave law which Congress passed while he was abroad. While in Europe, he studied medicine, and, after manumission, returned to America to practice medicine and to write.

In his own time, Brown was well-known for lectures and letters attacking slavery. These, however, represent only part of his voluminous and varied work. His first literary work was an auto-biography, *The Narrative of William W. Brown* (1847), which sold eight thousand copies within the first eight months after publication. A year later, he published a book of poems, *The Anti-Slavery Harp*. In 1852, he collected his letters into *My Three Years in Europe*, the first travel book by an Afro-American, and the following year, he published in London the first novel by a Negro

From *Three Years in Europe; or, Places I Have Seen and People I Have Met* (London: Gilpin, 1852).

American — *Clotel, or The President's Daughter*, the story of one of the mulatto daughters of Thomas Jefferson's housekeeper. Revised and published in America in 1864 as *Clotelle: A Tale of the Southern States*, with no mention of Jefferson, the novel became very popular among Union soldiers. In 1858, he wrote *The Escape, or a Leap for Freedom*, the first play by a Negro American. His last published works were collections of biographical-historical sketches: *The Black Man: His Antecedents, His Genius, and His Achievements* (1863), *The Negro in the American Rebellion: His Heroism and His Fidelity* (1867), *The Rising Son* (1874), and *My Southern Home, or The South and Its People* (1880).

The following is one of a series of letters which Brown wrote while traveling in Europe. Although Brown concerned himself largely with lyric descriptions of people and places, he could not forget the slavery from which he had escaped.

Letter XI

York Minster — The Great Organ — Newcastle-on-Tyne — The Labouring Classes — The American Slave —Sheffield—James Montgomery.

January, 1850.

Some days since, I left the Metropolis to fulfill a few engagements to visit provincial towns; and after a ride of nearly eight hours, we were in sight of the ancient city of York. It was night, the moon was in her zenith, and there seemed nothing between her and the earth but glittering gold. The moon, the stars, and the innumerable gas-lights, gave the city a panoramic appearance. Like a mountain starting out of a plain, there stood the Cathedral in all its glory, looking down upon the surrounding buildings, with all the appearance of a Gulliver standing over the Lilliputians. Night gave us no opportunity to view the Minster. However, we were up the next morning before the sun, and walking round the Cathedral with a degree of curiosity seldom excited within us. It is thought that a building of the same dimensions would take fifty years to complete it at the present time, even with all the improvements of the nineteenth century, and would cost no less than the enormous sum of two millions of pounds sterling. From what I had heard of this famous Cathedral, my expectations were raised to the highest point; but it surpassed all the ideas that I had formed of it. On entering the building, we lost all thought of the external appearance by the matchless beauty of the interior. The echo produced by the tread of our feet upon the floor as we entered, resounding through the aisles, seemed to say "Put off your shoes, for the place whereon you tread is holy ground." We stood with hat in hand, and gazed with wonder and astonishment down the incomparable vista of more than five hundred feet. The organ, which stands near the centre of the building, is said to be one of the finest in the world. A wall, in front of which is a screen of the most gorgeous and florid architecture and executed in solid stone, separates the nave from the service choir. The beautiful workmanship of this makes it appear so perfect, as almost to produce the belief that it is tracery work of wood. We ascended the rough stone steps through a winding stair to the turrets, where we had such a view of the surrounding country, as can be obtained from no other place. On the top of the centre and highest turret, is a grotesque figure of a fiddler; rather a strange looking object, we thought, to occupy the most elevated pinnacle on the house of God. All dwellings in the neighborhood appear like so many dwarfs couching at the feet of the Minster; while its own vastness and beauty impress the observer with feelings of awe and sublimity. As we stood upon the top of this stupendous mountain of ecclesiastical architecture, and surveyed the picturesque hills and valleys around, imagination recalled the tumult of the sanguinary battles fought in sight of the edifice. The rebellion of Octavius near three thousand years ago, his defeat and flight to the Scots, his return and triumph over the Romans and being crowned king of all Britain; the assassination of Oswald king of the Northumbrians; the flaying alive of Osbert; the crowning of Richard III; the siege by William the Conqueror; the siege by Cromwell, and the pomp and splendour with which the different monarchs had been received in York, all appeared to be vividly before me. While we were thus calling to our aid our knowledge of history, a sweet peal from the lungs of the ponderous organ below cut short our stay among the turrets, and we descended to have our organ of tune gratified, as well as to finish the inspection of the interior.

I have heard the sublime melodies of Handel, Hayden, and Mozart, performed by the most skilful musicians; I have listened with delight and awe to the soul-moving compositions of those masters, as they have been chaunted in the most magnificent churches; but never did I hear such music, and played upon such an instrument, as that sent forth by the great organ in the Cathedral of York. The verger took much delight in showing us the Horn that was once mounted with gold, but is now garnished with brass. We viewed the monuments and tombs of the departed, and then spent an hour before the great north window. The designs on the painted glass, which tradition states was given to the church by five virgin sisters, is the finest thing of the kind in Great Britain. I felt a relief on once more coming into the open air and again beholding Nature's own sun-light. The splendid ruins of St. Mary's Abbey, with its eight beautiful light gothic windows, next attracted our attention. A visit to the Castle finished our stay in York; and as we were leaving the old city we almost imagined that we heard the chiming of the bells for the celebration of the first Christian Sabbath, with Prince Arthur as the presiding genius.

   *   *   *   *   *   *

England stands pre-eminently the first government in the world for freedom of speech and of the press. Not even in our own beloved America, can the man who feels himself oppressed speak as he can in Great Britain. In some parts of England, however, the freedom of thought is tolerated to a greater extent than in others; and of the places favourable to reforms of all kinds, calculated to elevate and benefit mankind, Newcastle-on-Tyne doubtless takes the lead. Surrounded by innumerable coal mines, it furnishes employment for a large labouring population, many of whom take a deep interest in the passing events of the day, and, consequently, are a reading class. The public debater or speaker, no matter what may be his subject, who fails to get an audience in other towns, is sure of a gathering in the Music Hall, or Lecture Room in Newcastle. Here I first had an opportunity of coming in contact with a portion of the labouring people of Britain. I have addressed large and influential meetings in Newcastle and the neighboring towns, and the more I see and learn of the condition of the working-classes of England the more I am satisfied of the utter fallacy of the statements often made that their condition approximates to that of the slaves of America. Whatever may be the disadvantages that the British peasant labours under, he is free; and if he is not satisfied with his employer he can make choice of another. He also has the right to educate his children; and he is the equal of the most wealthy person before an English Court of Justice. But how is it with the American Slave? He has no right to himself, no right to protect his wife, his child, or his own person. He is nothing more than a living tool. Beyond his field or workshop he knows nothing. There is no amount of ignorance he is not capable of. He has not the least idea of the face of this earth, nor of the history or constitution of the country in which he dwells. To him the literature, science, and art — the progressive history, and the accumulated discoveries of byegone ages, are as if they had never been. The past is to him as yesterday, and the future scarcely more than to-morrow. Ancestral monuments, he has none; written documents fraught with cogitations of other times, he has none; and any instrumentality calculated to awaken and expound the intellectual activity and comprehension of a present or approaching generation, he has none. His condition is that of the leopard of his own native Africa. It lives, it propagates its kind; but never does it indicate a movement towards that all but angelic intelligence of man. The slave eats, drinks, and sleeps — all for the benefit of the man who claims his body as his property. Before the tribunals of his country he has no voice. He has no higher appeal than the mere will of his owner. He knows nothing of the inspired Apostles through their writings. He has no Sabbath, no Church, no Bible, no means of grace, — and yet we are told that he is as well off as the labouring classes of England. It is not enough that the people of my country should point to their Declaration of Independence which declares that "all men are created equal." It is not enough that they should laud to the skies a constitution containing boasting declarations in favour of freedom. It is not enough that they should extol the genius of Washington, the patriotism of Henry, or the enthusiasm of Otis. The time has come when nations are judged by the acts of the present instead of the past. And so it must be with America. In no place in the United Kingdom has the American Slave warmer friends than in Newcastle.

*   *   *   *   *   *

I am now in Sheffield, and have just returned from a visit to James Montgomery, the poet. In company with James Wall, Esq., I proceeded to The Mount, the residence of Mr. Montgomery; and our names being sent in, we were soon in the presence of the "Christian Poet." He held in his left hand the *Eclectic Review* for the month, and with the right gave me a hearty shake, and bade me "Welcome to old England." He was anything but like the portraits I had seen of him, and the man I had in my mind's eye. I had just been reading his "Pelican Island," and I eyed the poet with no little interest. He is under the middle size, his forehead high and well formed, the top of which was a little bald; his hair of a yellowish colour, his eyes rather small and deep set, the nose long and slightly acquiline, his mouth rather small, and not at all pretty. He was dressed in black, and a large white cravat entirely hid his neck and chin: his having been afflicted from childhood with saltrhum, was doubtless the cause of his chin being so completely buried in the neckcloth. Upon the whole, he looked more like one of our American Methodist parsons, than any one I have seen in this country. He entered freely into conversation with us. He said he should be glad to attend my lecture that evening, but that he had long since quit going out at night. He mentioned having heard William Lloyd Garrison some years before, and with whom he was well pleased. He said it had long been a puzzle to him, how Americans could hold slaves and still retain their membership in churches. When we rose to leave, the old man took my hand between his two, and with tears in his eyes said, "Go on your Christian mission, and may the Lord protect and prosper you. Your enslaved countrymen have my sympathy, and shall have my prayers." Thus ended our visit to the Bard of Sheffield. Long after I had quitted the presence of the poet, the following lines of his were ringing in my ears: —

> "Wanderer, whither dost thou roam?
> Weary wanderer, old and grey,
> Wherefore has thou left thine home,
> In the sunset of thy day.
> Welcome wanderer as thou art,
> All my blessings to partake;
> Yet thrice welcome to my heart,
> For thine injured people's sake.
> Wanderer, whither would'st thou roam?
> To what region far away?
> Bend thy steps to find a home,
> In the twilight of thy day.
> Where a tyrant never trod,
> Where a slave was never known —
> But where Nature worships God
> In the wilderness alone."

Mr. Montgomery seems to have thrown his entire soul into his meditations on the wrongs of Switzerland. The poem from which

we have just quoted, is unquestionably one of his best produc-
tions, and contains more of the fire of enthusiasm than all his
other works. We feel a reverence almost amounting to supersti-
tion, for the poet who deals with nature. And who is more capable
of understanding the human heart than the poet? Who has better
known the human feelings than Shakspere; better painted than
Milton, the grandeur of Virtue; better sighed than Byron over
the subtle weaknesses of Hope? Who ever had a sounder taste, a
more exact intellect than Dante? or who has ever tuned his harp
more in favour of Freedom, than our own Dante?

Frederick Douglass (1817-1895)

A Letter to Mrs. Stowe

Born a slave on the Eastern Shore of Maryland, Frederick Bailey became the best-known Negro of his generation. After escaping from slavery, Bailey, who had taught himself to read and to write, assumed the name of Douglass and was persuaded to work as an agent for the Massachusetts Anti-Slavery Society. One of the most gifted orators in a century which produced Daniel Webster and William Jennings Bryan, the handsome, muscular Douglass was so articulate that pro-slavery skeptics doubted that he had ever been a slave. To refute the allegation, he wrote *Narrative of the Life of Frederick Douglass* (1845), which he later expanded into *My Bondage and My Freedom* (1855) and *The Life and Times of Frederick Douglass* (1891). After a trip to England in 1845, where he was lionized, Douglass became increasingly disenchanted with William Lloyd Garrison and other members of the Massachusetts Anti-Slavery Society. He opposed their attempts to reject the Constitution as a pro-slavery document, and he argued for the use of direct political action as the most effective means of overthrowing slavery. Above all, however, he resented their attempts to restrict his speeches to a mere recitation of his experiences as a slave; he wanted the freedom to assist the Abolitionists in shaping the policy of the movement. In 1847,

From *The Mind of the Negro as Reflected in Letters Written during the Crisis,* edited by Carter G. Woodson (Lancaster, Pa.: Association for the Study of Negro Life and History, Inc., 1926). Reprinted with the permission of The Association for the Study of Negro Life and History.

he separated from the Massachusetts Society, and began publication of a weekly, *The North Star,* later known as *Frederick Douglass's Paper,* which lasted until 1860. From 1858 to 1863, he produced *Douglass's Monthly,* and from 1869 to 1872 he wrote another weekly, *New National Era.*

Although his major talent was his oratory, his many editorials and letters evidence his ability as a writer. In the following selection, somewhat atypical in its mildness, Douglass urges for the welfare of Negroes an industrial education, comparable to that advocated by Booker T. Washington later.

Letter to Mrs. Stowe

ROCHESTER, March 8, 1853

MY DEAR MRS. STOWE:

You kindly informed me, when at your house a fortnight ago, that you designed to do something which would permanently contribute to the improvement and elevation of the free coloured people in the United States. You especially expressed interest in such of this class as had become free by their own exertions, and desired most of all to be of service to them. In what manner and by what means you can assist this class most successfully, is the subject upon which you have done me the honour to ask my opinion. . . I assert then that *poverty, ignorance* and *degradation* are the combined evils; or in other words, these constitute the social disease of the free coloured people of the United States.

To deliver them from this triple malady, is to improve and elevate them, by which I mean, simply to put them on an equal footing with their white fellow countrymen in the sacred right to *"Life, Liberty,* and the pursuit of happiness." I am for no fancied or artificial elevation, but only ask fair play. How shall this be obtained? I answer, first, not by establishing for our use high schools and colleges. Such institutions are, in my judgment, beyond our immediate occasions and are not adapted to our present most pressing wants. High schools and colleges are excellent institutions, and will in due season be greatly subservient to our progress; but they are the result, as well as they are the demand of a point of progress, which we as a people have not yet attained. Accustomed as we have been, to the rougher and harder modes of living, and of gaining a livelihood, we cannot, and we ought not to hope that in a single leap from our low condition, we can reach that of

Minister, Lawyers, Doctors, Editors, Merchants, etc. These will doubtless be attained by us; but this will only be, when we have patiently and laboriously, and I may add, successfully, mastered and passed through the intermediate gradations of agriculture and the mechanical arts. Besides, there are — and perhaps this is a better reason for my view of this case — numerous institutions of learning in this country, already thrown open to coloured youth. To my thinking, there are quite as many facilities now afforded to the coloured people, as they can spare the time from the sterner duties of life, to avail themselves of. In their present condition of poverty, they cannot spare their sons and daughters two or three years at boarding-schools or colleges, to say nothing of finding the means to sustain them while at such institutions. I take it, there-fore, that we are well provided for in this respect; and that it may be fairly inferred from the fact, that the facilities for our education, so far as schools and colleges in the Free States are concerned, will increase quite in proportion with our future wants. Colleges have been open to coloured youth in this country during the last dozen years. Yet few comparatively, have acquired a classical education; and even this few have found themselves educated far above a living condition, there being no methods by which they could turn their learning to account. Several of this latter class have entered the ministry; but you need not be told that an educated people is needed to sustain an educated ministry. There must be a certain amount of cultivation among the people to sustain such a ministry. At present we have not that cultivation amongst us; and therefore, we value in the preacher, strong lungs, rather than high learning. I do not say, that educated ministers are not needed amongst us, far from it! I wish there were more of them! but to increase their number, is not the largest benefit you can bestow upon us.

We have two or three coloured lawyers in this country; and I rejoice in the fact, for it affords very gratifying evidence of our progress. Yet it must be confessed, that in point of success, our lawyers are as great failures as our ministers. White people will not employ them to the obvious embarrassment of their causes, and the blacks, taking their *cue* from the whites, have not suffi-cient confidence in their abilities to employ them. Hence educated coloured men, among the coloured people, are at a very great discount.

It would seem that education and emigration go together with us, for as soon as a man rises amongst us, capable, by his genius and learning, to do us great service, just so soon he finds that he can serve himself better by going elsewhere. In proof of this, I might instance the Russwurms, the Garnets, the Wards, the Crummells and others, all men of superior ability and attainments, and capable of removing mountains of prejudice against their race, by their simple presence in the country; but these gentlemen, finding themselves embarrassed here by the peculiar disadvantages to which I have referred, disadvantages in part growing out of their education, being repelled by ignorance on the one hand, and prejudice on the other, and having no taste to continue a contest against such odds, they have sought more congenial climes, where they can live more peaceable and quiet lives. I regret their election, but I cannot blame them; for with an equal amount of education and the hard lot which was theirs, I might follow their example. . . .

There is little reason to hope that any considerable number of the free coloured people will ever be induced to leave this country; even if such a thing were desirable. This black man — *un*like the Indian — loves civilization. He does not make very great progress in civilization himself but he likes to be in the midst of it, and prefers to share its most galling evils, to encountering barbarism. Then the love of the country, the dread of isolation, the lack of adventurous spirit, and the thought of seeming to desert their "brethren in bonds," are a powerful check upon all schemes of colonization, which look to the removal of the coloured people, without the slaves. The truth is, dear madam, we are *here*, and here we are likely to remain. Individuals emigrate—nations never. We have grown up with this republic, and I see nothing in her character, or even in the character of the American people as yet, which compels the belief that we must leave the United States. If then, we are to remain here, the question for the wise and good is precisely that you have submitted to me — namely: What can be done to improve the condition of the free people of colour in the United States?

The plan which I humbly submit in answer to this inquiry—and in the hope that it may find favour with you, and with the many friends of humanity who honour, love, and cooperate with you—is the establishment in Rochester, N. Y., or in some other part of the United States equally favourable to such an enterprise, of an INDUSTRIAL COLLEGE in which shall be taught several important branches of the mechanical arts. This college to be opened to coloured youth. I will pass over the details of such an institution as I propose. . . . Never having had a day's schooling in all my life I may not be expected to map out the details of a plan so comprehensive as that involved in the idea of a college. I repeat, then,

I leave the organisation and administration to the superior wisdom of yourself and the friends who second your noble efforts.

The argument in favour of an Industrial College — a college to be conducted by the best men — and the best workmen which the mechanical arts can afford; a college where coloured youth can be instructed to use their hands, as well as their heads; where they can be put into possession of the means of getting a living whether their lot in after life may be cast among civilized or uncivilized men; whether they choose to stay here, or prefer to return to the land of their fathers — is briefly this: Prejudice against the free coloured people in the United States has shown itself nowhere so invincible as among mechanics. The farmer and the professional man cherish no feeling so bitter as that cherished by these. The latter would starve us out of the country entirely. At this moment I can more easily get my son into a lawyer's office to learn law than I can into a blacksmith's shop to blow the bellows and to wield the sledge-hammer. Denied the means of learning useful trades we are pressed into the narrowest limits to obtain a livelihood. In times past we have been the hewers of wood and the drawers of water for American society, and we once enjoyed a monopoly in menial enjoyments, but this is so no longer. Even these enjoyments are rapidly passing away out of our hands. The fact is — every day begins with the lesson, and ends with the lesson—that coloured men must learn trades; and must find new employment; new modes of usefulness to society, or that they must decay under the pressing wants to which their condition is rapidly bringing them.

We must become mechanics; we must build as well as live in houses; we must make as well as use furniture; we must construct bridges as well as pass over them, before we can properly live or be respected by our fellow men. We need mechanics as well as ministers. We need workers in iron, clay, and leather. We have orators, authors, and other professional men, but these reach only a certain class, and get respect for our race in certain select circles. To live here as we ought we must fasten ourselves to our countrymen through their every day cardinal wants. We must not only be able to *black* boots, but to *make* them. At present we are unknown in the Northern States as mechanics. We give no proof of genius or skill at the county, State, or national fairs. We are unknown at any of the great exhibitions of the industry of our fellow-citizens, and being unknown we are unconsidered.

The fact that we make no show of our ability is held conclusive of our inability to make any, hence all the indifference and contempt with which incapacity is regarded, fall upon us, and that too, when we have had no means of disproving the infamous opinion of our natural inferiority. I have during the last dozen years denied before the Americans that we are an inferior race; but this has been done by arguments based upon admitted principles rather than by the presentation of facts. Now, firmly believing, as I do, that there are skill, invention, power, industry, and real mechanical genius, among the coloured people, which will bear favourable testimony for them, and which only need the means to develop them, I am decidedly in favour of the establishment of such a college as I have mentioned. The benefits of such an institution would not be confined to the Northern States, nor to the free coloured people. They would extend over the whole Union. The slave not less than the freeman would be benefited by such an institution. It must be confessed that the most powerful arguments now used by the Southern slaveholder, and the one most soothing to his conscience, is that derived from the low condition of the free coloured people of the North. I have long felt that too little attention has been given by our truest friends in this country to removing this stumbling block out of the way of the slave's liberation.

The most telling, the most killing refutation of slavery, is the presentation of an industrious, enterprising, thrifty, and intelligent free black population. Such a population I believe would rise in the Northern States under the fostering care of such a college as that supposed.

To show that we are capable of becoming mechanics I might adduce any amount of testimony; but dear madam, I need not ring the changes on such a proposition. There is no question in the mind of any prejudiced person that the negro is capable of making a good mechanic. Indeed, even those who cherish the bitterest feelings towards us have admitted that the apprehension that negroes might be employed in their stead, dictated the policy of excluding them from trades altogether. But I will not dwell upon this point as I fear I have already trespassed too long upon your precious time, and written more than I ought to expect you to read.

Allow me to say in conclusion, that I believe every intelligent coloured man in America will approve and rejoice at the establishment of some such institution as that now suggested. There are many respectable coloured men, fathers of large families, having boys nearly grown up, whose minds are tossed by day and by night with the anxious enquiry, "what shall I do with my boys?" Such an institution would meet the wants of such persons. Then, too, the establishment of such an institution would be in character with the eminently practical philanthropy of your trans-Atlantic friends. America could scarcely object to it as an attempt to agitate the public mind on the subject of slavery, or to *dissolve the Union*. It could not be tortured into a cause for hard words by the American people, but the noble and good of all classes would see in the effort an excellent motive, a benevolent object, temperately, wisely, and practically manifested.

Wishing, you, dear madam, renewed health, a pleasant passage, and safe return to your native land.

I am most truly, your grateful friend,

FREDERICK DOUGLASS.

Alexander Crummell (1819-1898)

The Negro Race not under a Curse

Alexander Crummell, an Episcopalian minister, was one of the intellectual leaders of Negroes during the last decades of the nineteenth century. His fame has diminished since his death, and today he is almost unknown, even among historians. In his time, however, he earned lavish praise from such distinguished contemporaries as William Wells Brown, who, in *Three Years in Europe*, recorded their meeting at Cambridge, and W. E. B. DuBois, whose eloquent tribute is printed in a later section of this book.

Born in New York City and educated in theology in Boston, Crummell received a Bachelor of Arts from Cambridge University (England) in 1853. After spending the next twenty years in Liberia, he returned to America to become rector at St. Paul's Episcopal Church in Washington, D. C.

Crummell's literary reputation depends largely upon three collections of essays and sermons — *The Future of Africa* (1862), *The Greatness of Christ, and Other Sermons* (1882), and *Africa and America* (1892). As a theologian, Crummell urged young Negroes to develop the moral strength to become teachers and leaders of the race. Frequently, however, topical issues compelled him to defend Negroes against unjust attacks.

In the following selection, which reveals his characteristic logic, directness, and precise style, Crummell refutes a popular justifi-

---

From *The Future of Africa*. (New York: Charles Scribner, 1862).

25

cation of slavery — the belief that it was a curse which Noah placed on Ham.

The Negro Race not under a Curse*

The chief object of this paper is to show the falsity of the opinion that the sufferings and the slavery of the Negro race are the consequence of the curse of Noah, as recorded in Genesis ix. 25. That this is a general, almost universal, opinion in the Christian world, is easily proven. During the long controversy upon the slavery question which has agitated Christendom, no argument has been so much relied upon, and none more frequently adduced. It was first employed in vindication of the lawfulness of the slave trade. When the slave trade was abolished, and philanthropists commenced their warfare against the system of slavery, the chief pro-slavery argument brought forward in support of that system was this text. The friends of the Negro race have had to meet it when asserted by statesmen in the Legislature, and they have had to contend against the earnest affirmation of it by learned divines. And now, although both slavery and the slave trade are condemned by the general sentiment of the Christian world, yet the same interpretation is still given to this text, and the old opinion which was founded on it still gains credit and receives support. Its insidious influence relaxes the missionary zeal of even many pious persons, who can see no hope for Africa, nor discover any end to the slavery of its sons. It is found in books written by learned men; and it is repeated in lectures, speeches, sermons, and common conversation. So strong and tenacious is the hold which it has taken upon the mind of Christendom, that it seems almost impossible to uproot it. Indeed,

---

*This paper was originally written as a letter, in reply to another from an eminent philanthropic lady in Cheltenham, England. She communicated it to the then Editor of the London "Christian Observer," in which monthly it was published in September, 1852. Subsequent to this, in compliance with the request of many persons, it was rewritten and prepared, in its present form, for publication as a tract. Perhaps the Author may be permitted to say here, that it has had the advantage of being read by the late Rev. G. Stanley Faber, D.D., of Sherburne, the distinguished author of many learned works, who expressed his approbation of it, and presented the writer with his learned and able work, "PROPHETICAL DISSERTATIONS," in which the writer found that Mr. Faber had, several years ago, taken the same view of Gen. ix. 25, as is contained in this article.

it is an almost foregone conclusion, that the Negro race is an accursed race, weighed down, even to the present, beneath the burden of an ancestral malediction. The prejudice against this race seems as wide, as absolute, and as decided, as that entertained by the Jews against the Samaritans.

2. The Opinions of Commentators and Theological Writers.

A very few references to writers in the past and at the present will show the prejudiced views of even eminently good men upon this topic. POOLE admits the primary and pointed application of the curse to Canaan; he also acknowledges the subsequent power and greatness of the other three sons of Ham, and the spiritual blessedness which ultimately attended them; yet, with singular inconsistency, in another place, he involves Ham, the father, in the curse, which he declares to have been pointed at his son Canaan. He says: "When Canaan is mentioned, *Ham* is not exempted from the curse, but rather more deeply plunged into it; whilst he is pronounced accursed, not only in his person, (which is manifestly supposed by his commission of that sin for which the curse was inflicted,) but also in his posterity, which doubtless was a great aggravation of his grief."*

The learned and pious MATTHEW HENRY says: "He (that is, Noah) pronounces a curse on Canaan, the son of Ham, in whom Ham himself is cursed; either because this son of his was now more guilty than the rest, or because the posterity of this son were afterward to be rooted out of their land, to make room for Israel."† Again, in another place, speaking of the division of the families of the earth, he says: "The birthright was now to be divided between Shem and Japheth, *Ham being utterly discarded.*"

BISHOP NEWTON, in the first place, applies this prophecy to Canaan and his descendants; but he afterward gives a fanciful correction of the text, on the authority of the Septuagint and the Arabic version; and then asks: "May we not suppose that the copyist, by mistake, wrote only *Canaan*, instead of *Ham, the father of Canaan*, and that the whole passage was originally thus: And Ham, the father of Canaan, saw the nakedness of his father,

---

*Poole on Gen. ix. 25.
†See Henry's Commentary on Gen. ix. 25.

&c. &c. And he said, Cursed be Ham, the father of Canaan, &c.?"
He then goes on to remark: "By this reading all the three sons
of Noah are included in the prophecy, whereas otherwise Ham,
who was the offender, is excluded, or is only punished in one of
his children. . . . . . . The whole continent of Africa was peopled
principally by the children of Ham; and for how many ages have
the better parts of that country lain under the dominion of the
Romans, and then of the Saracens, and now of the Turks! In
what wickedness, ignorance, barbarity, slavery, misery, live most
of the inhabitants! And of the poor Negroes, how many hundreds
every year are sold and bought like beasts in the market, and are
conveyed from one quarter of the world to do the work of beasts
in another! Nothing can be more complete than the execution of
the sentence upon *Ham*, as well as upon Canaan."*

The excellent Rev. THOMAS SCOTT says: "The frequent mention
of Ham as the father of Canaan, suggests the thought that the
latter was also criminal. . . . . . Ham must have felt it a very
mortifying rebuke, when his own father was inspired, on this
occasion, to predict the durable oppression and slavery of his
posterity; Canaan was also rebuked by learning that the curse
would especially rest on that branch of the family which would
descend from him; for his posterity were no doubt *principally*,
though not *exclusively*, intended. . . . . . True religion has hith-
erto flourished very little among Ham's descendants; they remain
to this day almost entire strangers to Christianity, and their
condition, in every age, has remarkably coincided with this
prediction."†

Similar views are expressed by KEITH, who remarks: "The
unnatural conduct of Ham, and the dutiful and respectful behavior of Shem and Japheth toward their aged father, gave rise
to the prediction of the future fate of their posterity, without
being at all assigned as the cause of that fate. . . . . Though long
banished from almost all Europe, slavery still lingers in Africa.
That country is distinguished, above every other, as the land of
slavery. Slaves at home, and transported for slavery, the poor
Africans, the descendants of Ham, are the servants of servants,
or slaves to others."‡

In a popular work much used in the schools and the universities
of England, this comment upon the curse of Noah is found:
These prophecies (Gen. ix. 25–27) have since been wonderfully

---

*See Newton on Prophecies, Dissertation I.
†Scott on Gen. ix. 24, 25.
‡See Keith on the Prophecies.

fulfilled; the Egyptians were afflicted with various plagues; the land of *Canaan*, eight hundred years afterward, was delivered by God into the hands of the Israelites under Joshua, who destroyed great numbers and obliged the rest to fly, some into Africa, and others into various countries; what their condition is in Africa, we know at this day."*

The Rev. Dr. CUMMING, of London, thus discourses upon this subject:

"Read the predictions respecting *Ham*, that his descendants, the children of Africa, should be bondsmen of bondsmen. England nobly sacrificed twenty millions, in order to wash her hands of the heinous crime and horrible abominations of slavery, and sent her cruisers to sweep the seas of every craft that ventured to encourage the inhuman traffic. But while God is not the author of sin, nor man irresponsible for his crimes, slavery has grown under all the attempts to extinguish it, and shot up in spite of the power of Britain and the piercing protest of outraged humanity, the hour of its extinction not having yet come; thereby showing that heaven and earth may pass away, but that one jot or tittle of God's word cannot pass away."†

3. The Real State of the Case.

The writer of this paper differs from the distinguished persons here referred to. He regards the prevalent opinions upon this subject a sad preversion of Biblical history on the part of the intelligent minds that have stereotyped them, during the last century and a half, in the literature and theology of the English language.

In considering this subject, there is one material point which should be carefully noticed — a point upon which nearly all writers upon the subject have greatly erred: THE CURSE WAS PRONOUNCED UPON CANAAN, NOT UPON HAM. "And he said, Cursed be Canaan, a servant of servants shall he be unto his brethren." Gen. ix. 25. This is the utterance of the Divine word, clear, plain, distinct. There may be differences of opinion as to the cause, the nature, the extent, the justice, and the influence of this judgment; but as it respects *the person* who is cursed, the word of God is

---

*Analysis of Scripture History, by Rev. W. H. Pinnock, B. C. L. *"What their condition is in Africa, we know at this day." Whose* condition? Some would suppose that Africa was peopled in the mass by Canaanites. Surely this is loose writing, and inaccurate history.

†Exeter Hall Lecture.

specific and pointed: "CURSED BE CANAAN;" and in this we have the curse, *direct*.

No one, indeed, can deny that learned and distinguished divines have thought that *Ham* fell under the dire influence of this strong malediction. The suppositions of such most eminent divines as Poole, and Henry, and Newton, have already been presented. But what are they when contrasted with the distinct and emphatic word of God? They *suppose* that Ham was cursed; the word of God says, "CURSED BE CANAAN."

But, as though the Holy Spirit intended that there should be no error or mistake in the matter, we find the curse upon Canaan repeated, that is, by implication, again and again, in this same chapter, (chap. ix.,) both in the context and sub-text. In the 18th verse of this (ix.) chapter it is written: "And the sons of Noah, that went forth of the ark, were Shem, and Ham, and Japheth; and *Ham is the father of Canaan.*" Why are Shem and Japheth spoken of *individually*, while Ham is mentioned *in relation to his son Canaan?* Why, there can be no doubt that this form of expression was *designed* to point out *Canaan* as a marked individual.

In verses 26 and 27 we find the same form of expression *twice*, "and Canaan shall be his servant." We now have the curse *indirect*. In both cases, however, it is manifest that Canaan was the person subjected to this curse. Neither directly nor indirectly is Ham, the father, denounced by Noah; and therefore we have the authority of the word of God, for the affirmation that the curse was *not* pronounced upon Ham.†

Now, in order to involve the Negro race in this malediction, one of two things must be proven: either,

1st. That Noah, in mentioning Canaan, intended to include *all* the children of Ham; or,

2d. That the Negro race, in Africa, are the descendants of Canaan.

---

* Mr. Faber asks, "Why Ham should be specially distinguished as the father of Canaan, while, *in the very same prophecy,* his two brothers are simply mentioned as Shem and Japheth, without any parallel genealogical adjunct to their names." See "Prophetical Dissertations:" Dis. ii. p. 102, note.

†In an old work entitled "The General History of the World," I find the following sentence: "Some have believed that Noah cursed Canaan because he could not well have cursed Ham himself, whom God had not long before blessed." And he refers to Sermon 29, Chrysostom in Genesis.

4. The Whole Family of Ham not Accursed.

It cannot be proven that *all* the sons of Ham were included in the curse pronounced upon Canaan. Ham had four sons: "And the sons of Ham, Cush, and Mizraim, and Phut, and Canaan." Gen. x. 6. Canaan, it is evident, was the *youngest* of these sons, and Cush the *eldest*.

Now, the common rule among men is that "THE GREATER INCLUDES THE LESS." If, therefore, Cush, the *eldest* of the sons of Ham, had been the person cursed, then there would have been some strength and plausibility in the plea, that, according to this principle, a curse upon him, that is, Cush, as the head and representative of the family, involved a curse upon his three younger brothers. But the curse was upon the youngest, *Canaan*. And there is no received rule among men, the reverse of that here quoted, that is, that "the less includes the greater."

So, also, if Ham himself had been the person designated by Noah, then all disputation upon this matter would be, at once, at an end; for then the inference would be natural, legitimate, and indisputable, that *all* his posterity were implicated in the curse which fell upon himself. But this fact is nowhere stated in Scripture. IT DOES, INDEED, RECORD GOD'S BLESSING UPON HAM AND HIS POSTERITY;* although this is universally passed over and ignored; but that he was cursed by Noah is only one of the conjectures of men. In the sacred record we find Canaan's name, and his only, mentioned as the person cursed.

It is mentioned, moreover, in such a way as though the Divine mind intended there should be a marked significance connected with it. For why, when the Scripture narrative is so careful to

---

* It is objected to the view taken, in this paper, of Gen. ix. 25, that Ham is left neither blessed nor cursed; and hence divines include him in the curse on Canaan. But it is a singular fact, that all the commentators neglect to notice the fact that Ham had just received a blessing from God.

In Genesis ix, 1, we read: "And God blessed Noah and his sons, and said unto them, Be fruitful," &c., &c. And in verses 8 and 12 it reads: "And God spake unto Noah, and to his sons *with him*, saying, And I, behold, I establish my covenant with you, and with your seed after you. . . . . . And God said, This is the token of the covenant which I make between me and you, and every living creature that is with you, *for perpetual generations*."

The question here arises "Does Noah's curse (*incidental to Ham's youngest son*) override the blessing of God, for perpetual generations, to Ham and his seed, in the general and particular blessings of Gen. ix. 9 and 12? Does the cure of *man* supersede and set aside the *covenanted* blessings of God?

give the names of Ham's four sons, according to seniority, why is *Canaan's name* — the name of the youngest — selected, singled out, and repeated, no less than *five* different times, in the brief narrative which records this remarkable event?* Surely for no other reason than to mark HIM distinctly as *the* individual referred to, and to separate his three elder brothers from the curse.

The argument of an American writer upon this point is of great force, and deserves notice. He adduces "two rules of law and logic, viz.: enumeration weakens, in cases not enumerated; exceptions strengthen, in cases not excepted. In the curse Canaan is enumerated, and therefore the probability of its application to his brothers is *weakened* by this enumeration, and in the blessings bestowed upon Shem and Japheth, in the next two verses, Canaan, and not Ham and his posterity, is excepted; and therefore the probability of the exclusive application of the curse to Canaan is strengthened by this exception."†

The testimony of Josephus accords with this theory. He says: "Noah spared Ham by reason of his nearness of blood, but cursed his posterity; and when the rest of them (*i. e.*, of the children of Ham) escaped that curse, God inflicted it on the children of Canaan.‡

This argument is strengthened and confirmed by a reference to the counterpart of this curse, which is seen in God's dealings with the Canaanites. It is seen in those severe commands to the Hebrews on their entrance into the promised land, to expel and destroy the devoted Canaanites. The indictment against this wicked and profane people is written, in fearfully descriptive terms, in the 18th chapter of Leviticus, which enumerates the aggravated crimes on account of which the Almighty was about calling them to judgment.§ The events which followed, in consequence of the commands of Jehovah to the Hebrews, have always been taken as the fulfilment of this prediction of Noah. By Jew and Christian Gentile, in the early periods of the Church, and in more recent times by writers upon prophecy, and by commentators upon the Bible, the havoc and destruction visited upon the Canaanites have been regarded, not only as a punishment for their wickedness, but also as the counterpart to the

---

* See Genesis ix, 18, 22, 25, 26, 27.

†I cannot give the name of the writer of the above. I found this extract in the fragment of a newspaper.

‡Josephus, "Antiquities of the Jews," B. i. Ch. vi.

§See Lev. xviii. 24–28.

prediction of Noah, and as a complete fulfilment of his prophetic curse upon Canaan.

To sum up, then, we have, for the application and *limitation* of this curse to Canaan and his posterity only, the following facts and arguments:

1. The text of Genesis.
2. Two fundamental rules of law and logic.
3. The testimony of Josephus.
4. The Scriptural account of the fate of the Canaanites.

5. The Negro Race not the Descendants of Canaan.

But, in reply to the above arguments, it may be said that, granting that the three elder sons of Ham were not under the curse, nevertheless the Negro race may be the descendants of Canaan, and hence under the infliction of this prophetic judgment.

The facts of the case warrant the most positive denial of the assertion that the Negro race are the descendants of Canaan. In fact, of all the sons of Ham, *Canaan was the only one who never entered Africa.* Of this there is abundant evidence, sacred and profane.

The evidence, so far as *Scripture* is concerned, is given us in Gen. x. 19: "And the border of the Canaanites was from Sidon, as thou comest to Gerar, unto Gaza; as thou goest unto Sodom and Gomorrah, and Admah, and Zeboim, even unto Lasha." The locality here designated is evidently the land of Palestine, and in Asia; and in the Pentateuch, this region is frequently called the land of Canaan.

A reference to the names of the descendants of Canaan will tend to place this still more distinctly before us. In Gen. x. 15–18, we find the following statement: "And Canaan begat Sidon, his first-born, and Heth, and the Jebusite, and the Amorite, and the Girgasite, and the Hivite, and the Arkite," &c., &c. These names, most surely, are not African, nor do they indicate African localities. We recognize in Sidon the name of that city, celebrated in history for its commerce and luxury, which stood on the Mediterranean, at the north of Palestine. The Hittites were the descendants of Heth, and lived in nearly the same quarter. The Jebusites were the descendants of Jebus, and their locality was the spot on which Jerusalem was built. And the Amorites, Girgasites, &c., are frequently mentioned in the Old Testament as inhabitants of the land of Canaan.

The *profane* historical evidence is brief, but clear, weighty, and decisive: it is the evidence of Josephus, who says: "Canaan, the fourth son of Ham, inhabited the country now called Judea, and called it, from his own name, Canaan."*

It appears, then, from the evidence adduced, that this curse, in its *significance* and LOCALITY, is altogether Asiatic, and not African. Asia was the field on which the Canaanites moved, and whence their history is derived. The Canaanites of old were Asiatics, that is, so far as residence is concerned; and the mass of their descendants, if existing anywhere, are the modern Syrians.

Again, the above facts and arguments may be opposed by some, by the fact that *some* of the Canaanites established themselves on the north coast of Africa, in a colony. But it is quite evident that the Negro race, which mostly peoples that vast continent, could not have proceeded from them: —

1. Because the establishment of Carthage, the great Phœnician (Canaanitish) colony, was at a late period in the history of the world;† but the permanent division of races had been formed centuries anterior to this event; and the Negro race, as a race, had long before sprung into existence.

2. If this were not the case, the probability is that the great desert would have prevented their being mingled with the mass of the aborigines who live south of the desert; and it is almost certain that the interior of Africa was first reached by the way of Egypt.

3. History informs us that Carthage, a colony, grew up, *by itself*, in one locality; flourished for a space, and then sank to decay; while it does *not* inform us that Carthage was the mother of nations, the founder of a race.

Moreover, the fact should not be forgotten that the blood of the Canaanites was more mingled with that of Europeans than with Africans; for they formed *more* colonies in Europe than in Africa, and their influence was stronger in Europe than in Africa; and they have left behind more numerous marks and monuments of their power in Europe than in Africa. Indeed, almost every vestige of their former might, in Africa, has been obliterated.

When the Israelites entered the promised land, they broke up the political establishment of the Canaanites, destroyed large

---

* Josephus, "Antiquities of the Jews," B. i. Ch. vi.

†The foundation of Carthage, Utica, Septis, &c., took place, according to Heeren, between 1000–500 B. C. See "Heeren's Historical Researches," Vol. i. Ch. ii.

numbers of them, and drove many of them out of the land. These latter went northward, and at first settled in the country called Phœnicia; and from this they received the name Phœnicians. And here it was that the Canaanites gave evidence of being a wonderfully active, enterprising, ingenious, and intellectual people — as much, if not more so, than any people of ancient times. They were a maritime nation, and their adventurous spirit led to the far regions of the North, and southward around the Cape of Good Hope, which they doubled, traversing thence the countries bordering on the Indian Ocean.* They had commercial intercourse all through the Mediterranean Sea. Their ships aand trade reached all along the coast of Europe, even beyond the pillars ot Hercules, to Britain and Ireland In many of thooo placcs they planted colonies, on both sides of the Mediterranean; carrying with them arts, letters, commerce, and civilization, to people yet rude and uncultivated. It appears to be an established fact that one of their colonies was planted on the coasts of both Spain and Ireland; and thus some of the Celts of the present day may now have some of the blood of the Canaanites flowing through their veins.†

"The establishment of a Canaanitish colony on the coast of Africa is no more evidence that the African race proceeded from Canaan, than the similar fact in Ireland and Spain is evidence that Europeans had such an origin.

6. Whence is the Origin of the Negro Race?

Here it may be well to give a passing notice to the question, Who were the progenitors of the Negro race?

The writer of this paper does not pretend to speak with certainty upon this question. The following, he thinks, is a true statement of the matter.

Africa was originally settled by the descendants of Ham, *excepting hio oon Oanaan.* Ham himself is supposed to have emigrated to Egypt; and Egypt, in Scripture, is called the "land of Ham."‡ There he attained to state and eminence; and after his death, it is said, was deified by his descendants. The supreme deity AM of the Egyptians, it is stated, signifies his name; e. g., (H)AM; and the Jupiter AMMON, in honor of whom a temple was erected, is supposed to indicate HAM.

---

* See Heeren's Historical Researches, Vol. i. Ch. iii.
† See Heeren's Historical Researches, Vol. i. Ch. ii. Also, Ezekiel xxvii.
‡Ps. cvi. 22.

Africa was peopled by Ham in the line of his *three* sons, CUSH, MIZRAIM, and PHUT.

1. Cush, the eldest, and undoubtedly the most distinguished of all the sons of Ham, appears to have been the great progenitor of the Negro race. His name is also associated, with distinction, with Asia. The records of these early periods of the world's history are by no means clear and distinct; but Cush appears to have gone, at first, into Arabia, between the Euphrates and the Tigris, the country sometimes called Chaldea, and in Scripture, Shiraz. Thence his descendants spread themselves abroad through the beautiful and luxuriant region of "Araby the blest," and eastward, by the Persian Gulf, to the Orient. Here, in the first place, Cush and his children distinguished themselves. Here Nimrod, his son, became the first of kings, and reared up the mighty city of Babylon, and founded Nineveh. In the course of time some of the descendants of Cush crossed the Straits of Babelmandel, turned their steps southward toward the source of the Nile, and settled in the land south of the Mountains of the Moon; and from them the Negro race has sprung, although the Cushites were, undoubtedly, greatly mingled in blood with the children of Mizraim and Phut.

2. Mizraim was the father of the Egyptians. Wherever, in our version, we find the name Egypt, in the original it is Mizraim.

3. Of Phut, the *third* son of Ham, we have but little more than conjecture. It is the generally received opinion that his descendants settled on the northern Atlantic coast of Africa — Libya, and the adjacent parts, the country of the Moors.

7. Slavery not Peculiar to the Negro Race.

But there may be persons who will still object that the severities of the African slave trade, and the horrors of Negro slavery, are peculiar and significant, indicate something special in their inflictions, outweigh all theory and argument, and give strength and authority to the opinion that the curse was pronounced upon Ham, and that the children of Africa have participated in its consequences. The reply to this is:

1st. That the severities of the African slave trade, and the horrors of Negro slavery, as exhibited in European colonies and possessions, are entirely *modern* — confined to a short period in the history of the world, and therefore not a true exemplification of the *general* condition of the Negro race.

2dly. That while it is true that servitude and slavery have existed in some form throughout Africa, in every stage of its history, it is also true that *servitude and slavery have been the general condition of society, in all nations, in all countries, at all periods of time,* and are not in any manner peculiar to the black man, or the Negro race.

In connection with this fact:

3dly. That if the general existence of slavery in a race, or among a people, is to be taken as an indication that a curse has descended upon them, then the mass of the Turks, Poles, Russians, Circassians, are lineal descendants of Canaan, and therefore "doomed races." And in the same category the larger portion of even Anglo-Saxons must be placed; for, but a short time since, a multitude of Britons were absolutely "goods and chattels," under the name of "villeins."

8. The Universal Prevalence of Slavery.

Those persons, surely, display great ignorance, who associate the system of slavery, specially and alone, with the Negro race, and who are not aware of its existence in other races, and in all periods of history. There are no people, whether ancient or modern, with whom slavery has not been, at one period or other, a national institution. Indeed, how very little freedom has ever been enjoyed in this sin-ridden world of ours! Among the various evils to which society has been subjected, none have been more general or more deadly than slavery. No portion of the globe has been exempt from this curse. Slavery existed among all the nations of antiquity of whom we have any knowledge. It was maintained among the Assyrians and Babylonians. That slavery existed among the Egyptians is evidenced by the testimony of the Bible. Joseph was sold by his brethren; and sold again to an officer of Pharaoh's household. The Canaanites, after they were driven from the land of Canaan, and set up empire in Tyre and Sidon, trafficked in the bodies of men. The Greeks and Romans held vast numbers of slaves; they were great traders in human flesh, and distinguished themselves beyond all other people as cruel slave-holders; they kept their slaves in the deepest subjection, and visited upon them the most horrible cruelties, as is instanced in the condition of the Helots.

In more recent times, we see the same prevalence of slavery among the nations. The whole western part of Europe, not long since, was in a state of abject vassalage. In Russia, twenty millions of serfs, even *now*, in wretchedness and poverty, suffer the infliction of the knout, and are subject to irresponsible power and unrestrained tyranny. And if all the truth were known, it would, no doubt, be seen, that some of the convulsions which have recently occurred on the continent, were, in fact, insurrections of slaves battling for personal freedom.

The same state of things has existed even in England. A few centuries since, Saxons were bought and sold in Ireland and Rome. At one time slaves and cattle were a kind of currency in the land; and down to the period of the Reformation, human beings were "marketable commodities."

In the light of these facts, how ignorant and idle is it to regard the children of Africa as the subjects of a peculiar curse, because, in the mysterious providence of God, they have participated in the miseries and the sufferings of a cruel system, which has existed from the dawn of history, *in every quarter of the globe*, among every people under the sun.*

9. The Cause of the Slave Trade, and of Negro Slavery in Christian Countries.

It was the discovery of America, and the development of the treasures of the New World, which led to all the accumulated horrors of the slave trade, and the dreadful barbarities of Negro slavery, in Christian lands. The system took its rise in the sixteenth century. Since then the shameful fact has been witnessed, by earth and by heaven, of men, civilized men, men born and reared in Christian lands and under Christian influences, tearing their fellow-creatures from home, and friends, and country; carrying them across the wide ocean; trading in the flesh and blood of human beings! The system of slavery, *as thus marked and distinguished*, is a MODERN affair—was unknown anterior to the discovery of America; and therefore, as such, not a fact of history —not the general, universal state of the Negro race.

10. The Slave Trade Doubly Disastrous.

But it should be remembered that this event did not bring distress and slavery upon the Negro race only; it struck at once,

---

* With reference to the general prevalence of the system of slavery, see a very able article in the "Life and Remains of Rev. B. B. Edwards, D. D.," late of Andover Theological Seminary.

with deadly, blasting influence, upon two races of men,—the Indian as well as the Negro; and if, because of its destructive and enslaving influence, we are to infer a people's descent from Canaan, then the American Indian is of his seed, as well as the Negro. So soon as the European planted his foot upon the western continent, he seized upon the aborigine as his instrument and property. Before there was any thought of stealing the African and making him a slave, the Indian was enslaved and over-worked; until, at last, he sank down, spent and overwearied, into the grave. And then, when the Indian was exterminated, the Negro was torn from his native land, brought across the water, and made to supply the red man's place. It is difficult to tell which has suffered the more from the discovery, and the slavery which has grown out of it—the Indian or the African. "In the West Indies," to use the words of another, "the whole native population became speedily extinct; the ten millions of that almost unearthly race, the gentle Caribs, vanished like a morning mist before their oppressors. They bled in war; they wasted away in the mines; they toiled to death in the sugar mills."* And then, when their spirits had fled from earthly thraldom, the "conquerors of the New World" turned toward the vast African continent for new victims to fill up the places they had made vacant by their murderous treatment of the natives.

11. Whence this Perversion of Scripture?

A consideration of this subject would be altogether incomplete, without an attempt to account for the origin of this perversion of the word of God, that is, that the Negro race is under a curse, and devoted to slavery. The writer of this article is fully aware of the responsibility he assumes in making the assertions which follow; but it is his deliberate conviction that this perversion of Scripture originated,

1st. In the unscriptural dogma, still maintained by Christian men, and even ministers, that slavery is consistent with, nay,

---

*Rev. J. S. Stone, D.D.

"Las Casas and Vieyra might be quoted to show the cruelties which stimulated them in their unwearied efforts to save the original inhabitants from servitude. The Indians vanished from the scene, giving way to a more enduring race, who were thenceforward to monopolize the miseries of slavery."—"Friends in Council," p. 121.

authorized by, the word and will of God, and that it existed among
the Jews under the divine sanction.*

2d. In the natural disposition of our corrupt nature to justify
a committed wrong, and, if possible, to claim the authority of
God's word for it; and this is the peculiarity which characterizes
this great and deep-seated error. It had its origin in the rise and
influence of the system of slavery; and this system has appropri-
ated for itself no stronger support than this, and those other
staple arguments, wrenched from the Scripture to vindicate and
sustain the whole fabric of Negro slavery.

Christianity, in the abstract, is a pure and perfect gift from
God to man. But Christianity is a deposit from heaven, in the
hands of sinful men; and consequently, in all its ages, Christianity
has suffered the loss which is the natural result of being entrusted
to this agency, and of being transmitted through this medium.
History proves this; for no one need be told that Christianity, in
every age, has partaken of the prevailing spirit of that age, whatever it might be. In a philosophical age, it has been influenced by
the philosophical spirit and dogmas of that age. In the middle
ages, Christianity was influenced by scholasticism. In the age
of wars and crusades, she produced Peter the Hermit, and her
prelates led forth mighty armies to battle. In an age of luxury,
its rigid tone has been relaxed by the enervating influence of
wealth, and ease, and refinement. That Christianity has suffered
in a like manner, in a slave-trading and a slave-holding age, no
one need wonder who looks at the wide and withering influence
which the slave trade and slavery have exerted, in all the countries
of Christendom, during the last three hundred years. During this
period, nearly all the literature of the chief European nations was
a Negro-hating and a pro-slavery literature. The institution of
slavery, wielding a most potent and commanding authority,
brought every thing, in politics, science, philosophy, and letters,
to bear in support of the slave trade, in maintenance of the institution of slavery, and to uphold the dogma that the Negro was but

---

*The mind of God upon this subject, so far as the *Old Testament* is concerned, is thus expressed in Exodus xxi. 16: "He that stealeth a man, and
selleth him, or if he be found in his hand, he shall surely be put to death."
Can any thing be more explicit?

So far as the *New Testament* is concerned, one distinct, unambiguous
and positive utterance would seem to be sufficient. St. Paul furnishes us
with such an one in 1 Timothy i. 9, 10: "Knowing this, that the law is not
made for a righteous man, but for . . . . . . MENSTEALERS"—$\alpha\nu\delta\rho o\pi\alpha\delta\iota\sigma\tau\alpha\iota s$.
See "Conybeare and Howson" upon this verse.

an inferior animal. The aid of science was invoked; philosophy trimmed her lamps; literature poured forth whatever treasures she could possibly command. The period has but recently passed since distinguished men in England and France exercised the keenest wit and the subtlest genius to prove that the Negro differed physically from the rest of the human species, and had a *distinct* organization. The puzzling questions concerning the cuticle, the coloring membrane, the "woolly" hair, the facial angle, the pelvis, and all the other supposed characteristic differences of the Negro race, have only recently been settled in a sensible, reasonable manner. In such a state of public sentiment in the Christian world, what wonder that the Church herself should have become tainted and infected by the deadly touch of slavery? And she did not escape; she, too, fell into the common sentiment of the age; and has not yet entirely unschooled herself from it;* and hence it was that, to a very considerable extent, for nigh three centuries, the black man has had a pro-slavery theology pressing him to the earth, as well as the all-grasping cupidity of man:

> "Trade, wealth, and fashion asked him still to bleed,
> And holy men gave Scripture for the deed."

To this prevailing sentiment we owe the fact that nearly all interpretations of Scripture, commentaries, works on prophecy, dissertations on Jewish servitude, sermons and theological treatises elicited by the anti-slavery struggle in England and America, nearly all are pervaded by a pro-slavery tone.

In legal matters it is an assumed principle "that in doubtful cases the advantage of the law shall be in favor of the prisoner;" but Christian men have reversed this principle, and in their treatises have assumed, as a foregone conclusion, that the spirit of the Bible was in favor of slavery, and *not* for freedom, and hence ingenuity has been exhausted in order to show the exact similitude between Jewish servitude and Negro slavery; and to prove that when Noah cursed Canaan he was looking right down the track of time upon some fine specimens of "Ebony," in the barracoons of the Gallinas, or some "fat and sleek" Negroes in the slave-shambles of Virginia!

---

* See, as a most lamentable instance, a recent scriptural defense of Negro slavery, by the venerable Rt. Rev. Bishop Hopkins, of Vermont.

Conclusion.

In conclusion, the author submits that the preceding examination authorizes the following conclusions:

1. That the curse of Noah was *pronounced* upon Canaan, *not* upon Ham.

2. That it *fell* upon Canaan, and was designed to fall upon him only.

3. That neither Ham, nor any of his three sons, was involved in this curse.

4. That the Negro race have not descended from Canaan; were never involved in the curse pronounced upon him; and their peculiar sufferings, during the last three centuries, are not the results or evidences of *any* specific curse upon them.

5. That the fact of slavery in the Negro race is not peculiar to them as a people; but a *general* evil existing in the whole human family; in which, in God's providence, the Negro family have latterly been called to suffer greatly, and doubtless for some high and important ends.

6. That the geographical designations of Scripture are to be taken in good faith; and that when the *"land of Canaan"* is mentioned in the Bible, it was not intended to include the Gold Coast, the Gaboon, Goree, or Congo.

This examination furnishes us with suggestions upon a few *collateral* subjects which have been more or less associated with, or deduced from, the false interpretation thus noticed:

1. We see that *whatever* may be the significance of Gen. ix. 25, *it does not imply mental degradation and intellectual inaptitude.* The curse of Noah did not rob Canaan and his descendents of their brains. The history of the Phœnicians gives evidence of as great creative faculty, and of as much mental force and energy, as that of any other people in the world. It would seem that they, of all the ancient world, were only *second* to the Romans in that commanding national influence which begets life in distant quarters, starts enterprise in new regions, and reproduces its own force and energy among other peoples. Of course, it follows legitimately from the above, that the *whole* Hamitic family are under no Divine doom to perpetual ignorance or endless moral benightedness.

2. The history of the Canaanites serves to show that the *"principle of chattelism"* is not the correlative of the curse of *Canaan;* this was neither their doom nor their destiny. Neither

in sacred nor profane history do we find them bought and sold like cattle. Driven out of Canaan, they themselves traded in "the bodies and souls" of men, but *not* so others with them.* The nearest approach to any thing of this character is the condition of the Gibeonites, who deceived Joshua; but their condition was that of *servants*.† Although subjugated and humbled, yet their personal and family rights were preserved intact, and none of the aggravations of slavery were permitted to reach themselves or their children. When set upon, at times, by lawless and ruthless men, both Divine and human power interposed for their protection and preservation.

3. This examination *nullifies the foolish notion that the curse of Canaan carried with it the sable dye which marks the Negro races of the world*. The descendants of Canaan in Palestine, Phœnicia, Carthage, and in their various colonies, were not black. They were not Negroes, either in lineage or color.

---

* See Ezekiel xxvii.
† See Joshua ix. 21. 2 Samuel xxi, 3, 4, 5, 6.

Paul Laurence Dunbar (1872-1906)

Negro Life in Washington

At the beginning of the twentieth century, Paul Laurence Dunbar was one of America's most popular poets. The first Negro American to earn and sustain an international reputation as a creative writer, he was highly praised by critics who pointed to him as a symbol of the intellectual and creative potential of the Negro race.

Born in Dayton, Ohio, a son of former slaves, Dunbar was educated at the same high school attended by Orville and Wilbur Wright. There he was elected president of the literary society and editor of the school newspaper. After graduation, he took a job as elevator operator, the best paying position he could obtain. While holding that position, he published his first book of poetry, *Oak and Ivy* (1892). In 1896, he attracted national attention with the publication of *Lyrics of Lowly Life*, his third book of poetry, for which William Dean Howells wrote an introduction in which he praised Dunbar as the first American Negro to evidence innate talent as a writer. In the ten remaining years of his life, Dunbar published three additional collections of poems, four novels, four collections of stories, and numerous articles and sketches.

Although his interest and talents were best revealed in his poetry, Dunbar, like many other celebrated personalities, frequently was asked to write his impressions of places, people, and events. He professed to dislike such work, but accepted it because it frequently paid better than poetry did. Despite his aesthetic

From *Harper's Weekly*, XLIV (January 13, 1900).

disinterest in essays, Dunbar generally infused them with the
light touches of satire and sentiment which characterize his best
writing.

The following selection reveals Dunbar's deftness in word
portraits and his desire to preserve the character traits which
he identified with the racial identity of the Negro.

Negro Life in Washington

Washington is the city where the big men of little towns come
to be disillusioned. Whether black or white, the little great soon
seek their level here. It matters not whether it is Ezekiel Corncray
of Podunk Center, Vermont, or Isaac Johnson of the Alabama
black belt—in Washington he is apt to come to a realization of
his true worth to the world.

In a city of such diverse characteristics it is natural that the
life of any portion of its people should be interesting. But when
it is considered that here the experiment of sudden freedom has
been tried most earnestly, and, I may say, most successfully, upon
a large percentage of the population, it is to the lives of these
people that one instinctively turns for color, picturesqueness, and
striking contrast.

It is the delicately blended or boldly differentiated light and
shade effects of Washington negro life that are the despair of
him who tries truthfully to picture it.

It is the middle-class negro who has imbibed enough of white
civilization to make him work to be prosperous. But he has not
partaken of civilization so deeply that he has become drunk and
has forgotten his own identity. The church to him is still the
centre of his social life, and his preacher a great man. He has
not—and I am not wholly sorry that he has not—learned the
repression of his emotions, which is the mark of a high and dry
civilization. He is impulsive, intense, fervid, and—himself. He
has retained some of his primitive ingenuousness. When he goes to
a party he goes to enjoy himself and not to pose. If there be
onlookers outside his own circle, and he be tempted to pose, he
does it with such childlike innocence and good-humor that no
one is for a moment anything but amused, and he is forgiven his
little deception.

Possibly in even the lower walks of life a warmer racial color
is discoverable. For instance, no other race can quite show the

counterpart of the old gentleman who passes me on Sunday on his way to church. An ancient silk hat adorns a head which I know instinctively is bald and black and shiny on top; but the edges are fringed with a growth of crisp white hair, like a frame around the mild old face. The broadcloth coat which is buttoned tightly around the spare form is threadbare, and has faded from black to gray-green; but although bent a little with the weight of his years, his glance is alert, and he moves briskly along, like a character suddenly dropped out of one of Page's stories. He waves his hand in salute, and I have a vision of Virginia of fifty years ago.

A real bit of the old South, though, as one sees it in Washington, is the old black mammy who trundles to and fro a little baby-carriage with its load of laundry-work, but who tells you, with manifest pride, "Yes, suh, I has nussed, off'n on, mo'n a dozen chillun of de X fambly, an' some of de men dat's ginuls now er in Cong'ess was jes nachully raised up off'n me." But she, like so many others, came to Washington when it was indeed the Mecca for colored people, where lay all their hopes of protection, of freedom, and of advancement. Perhaps in the old days, when labor brought better rewards, she saved something and laid it by in the ill-fated Freedman's Savings Bank. But the story of that is known; so the old woman walks the streets to-day, penniless, trundling her baby-carriage, a historic but pathetic figure.

Some such relic of the past, but more prosperous withal, is the old lady who leans over the counter of a tiny and dingy restaurant on Capitol Hill and dispenses coffee and rolls and fried pork to her colored customers. She wears upon her head the inevitable turban or handkerchief in which artists delight to paint the old mammies of the South. She keeps unwavering the deep religious instinct of her race, and is mighty in her activities on behalf of one or the other of the colored churches. Under her little counter she always has a contribution-book, and not a customer, white or black, high or low, who is not levied upon to "he'p de chu'ch outen hits 'stress." But one who has sat and listened to her, as, leaning chin on hand, she recounted one of her weird superstitious stories of the night-doctors and their doings, or the "awful jedgement on a sinnah man," is not unwilling to be put at some expense for his pleasure.

The old lady and her stories are of a different cast from that part of the Washington life which is the pride of her proudest people. It is a far cry from the smoky little restaurant on the Hill, with its genial and loquacious old owner, to the great business

block on Fourteenth Street and its wealthy, shrewd, and cultivated proprietor.

Colored men have made money here, and some of them have
known how to keep it. There are several of them on the Board
of Trade—five, I think—and they are regarded by their fellows
as solid, responsible, and capable business men. The present assess-
ment law was drafted by a colored member of the board, and
approved by them before it was submitted to Congress.

As for the professions, there are so many engaged in them that
it would keep one busy counting or attempting to count the dark-
skinned lawyers and doctors one meets in a day.

The cause of this is not far to seek. Young men come here to
work in the departments. Their evenings are to a certain extent
free. It is the most natural thing in the world that they should
improve their time by useful study. But why such a preponder-
ance in favor of the professions, you say. Are there not other useful pursuits—arts and handicrafts? To be sure there are. But then
your new people dearly love a title, and Lawyer Jones sounds well,
Dr. Brown has an infinitely more dignified ring, and as for Professor—well, that is the acme of titular excellence, and there are
more dark professors in Washington than one could find in a
day's walk through a European college town.

However, it is well that these department clerks should carry
something away with them when they leave Washington, for their
condition is seldom financially improved by their sojourn here.
This, though, is perhaps apart from the aim of the present article,
for it is no more true of the negro clerks than of their white
confrères. Both generally live up to the limit of their salaries.

The clerk has much leisure, and is in consequence a society
man. He must dress well and smoke as good a cigar as an Eastern
Congressman. It all costs money, and it is not unnatural that at
the end of the year he is a little long on unreceipted bills and short
on gold. The tendency of the school-teachers, now, seems to be
entirely different. There are a great many of them here, and on
the average they receive less than the government employés. But
perhaps the discipline which they are compelled to impart to their
pupils has its salutary effect upon their own minds and impulses.
However that may be, it is true that the banks and building
associations receive each month a part of the salaries of a large
proportion of these instructors.

The colored people themselves have a flourishing building association and a well-conducted bank, which do part—I am sorry
I cannot say the major part—of their race's business.

The influence which the success of a few men will have upon a whole community is indicated in the spirit of venture which actuates the rising generation of this city. A few years ago, if a man secured a political position, he was never willing or fit to do anything else afterward. But now the younger men, with the example of some of their successful elders before them, are beginning to see that an easy berth in one of the departments is not the best thing in life, and they are getting brave enough to do other things. Some of these ventures have proven failures, even disasters, but it has not daunted the few, nor crushed the spirit of effort in them.

It has been said, and not without some foundation in fact, that a colored man who came to Washington never left the place. Indeed, the city has great powers of attracting and holding its colored population; for, belong to whatever class or condition they may, they are always sure to find enough of that same class or condition to make their residence pleasant and congenial. But this very spirit of enterprise of which I have spoken is destroying the force of this dictum, and men of color are even going so far as to resign government positions to go away and strike out for themselves. I have in mind now two young men who are Washingtonians of the Washingtonians, and who have been in office here for years. But the fever has taken them, and they have voluntarily given up their places to go and try their fortunes in the newer and less crowded West.

Such things as these are small in themselves, but they point to a condition of affairs in which the men who have received the training and polish which only Washington can give to a colored man can go forth among their fellows and act as leaveners to the crudity of their race far and wide.

That the pleasure and importance of negro life in Washington are overrated by the colored people themselves is as true as that it is underrated and misunderstood by the whites. To the former the social aspect of this life is a very dignified and serious drama. To the latter it is nothing but a most amusing and inconsequential farce. But both are wrong: it is neither the one thing nor the other. It is a comedy of the period played out by earnest actors, who have learned their parts well, but who on that very account are disposed to mouth and strut a little and watch the gallery.

Upon both races the truth and significance of the commercial life among the negroes have taken a firmer hold, because the sight of their banks, their offices, and places of business are evidences which cannot be overlooked or ignored.

As for the intellectual life, a university set on a hill cannot be hid, and the fact that about this university and about this excellent high-school clusters a community in which people, unlike many of the educational fakirs which abound, have taken their degrees from Cambridge, Oxford, Edinburgh, Harvard, Yale, Cornell, Wellesley, and a score of minor colleges, demands the recognition of a higher standard of culture among people of color than obtains in any other city.

But, taking it all in all and after all, negro life in Washington is a promise rather than a fulfilment. But it is worthy of note for the really excellent things which are promised.

William Edward Burghardt DuBois (1868-1963)

Of the Passing of the First-Born *and* Of Alexander Crummell

Frequently a controversial figure, W. E. B. DuBois was a perceptive interpreter and outspoken champion of Negroes. Born in Great Barrington, Massachusetts, DuBois received the Bachelor of Arts degree from Fisk, and the Doctor of Philosophy from Harvard (1895), where his dissertation was *The Suppression of the African Slave Trade to the United States of America.* In 1896, he became professor of history and economics at Atlanta University, where he initiated and edited *Studies of Negro Problems,* which earned him recognition as the first Negro scientific student of history and sociology. More overtly aggressive than Booker T. Washington, DuBois gained national attention by leading opposition to Washington's conciliatory political and educational philosophies. One of the founders of the National Association for the Advancement of Colored People and the first editor of *The Crisis,* the official publication of that organization, DuBois, throughout his life, attempted to promote unity among all the colored peoples of the world. In his later years, he renounced his American citizenship and moved to Ghana, where he died.

Although he wrote novels, autobiographies, and histories, DuBois's literary talent is most effectively displayed in his essays, which range in style from lucid, tightly organized arguments to lyric and rambling expressions of personal emotions. The extensive range of his mind and style appears in the many editorials and articles which he wrote for *The Crisis,* in *The Gift of Black Folk*

From *The Souls of Black Folk.* (New York: McClurg, 1903).

(1924), and in *Dusk of Dawn* (1940). His major literary achievement, however, is *The Souls of Black Folk*, a very perceptive presentation of the temperaments and culture of Negroes. In the following selection from that work, DuBois, grieving over the loss of his son, reaches a bitter consolation.

Of the Passing of the First-Born

O sister, sister, thy first-begotten,
The hands that cling and the feet that follow,
The voice of the child's blood crying yet,
Who hath remembered me? who hath forgotten?
Thou hast forgotten, O summer swallow,
But the world shall end when I forget.

SWINBURNE.

"Unto you a child is born," sang the bit of yellow paper that fluttered into my room one brown October morning. Then the fear of fatherhood mingled wildly with the joy of creation; I wondered how it looked and how it felt, — what were its eyes, and how its hair curled and crumpled itself. And I thought in awe of her, — she who had slept with Death to tear a man-child from underneath her heart, while I was unconsciously wandering. I fled to my wife and child, repeating the while to myself half wonderingly, "Wife and child? Wife and child?" — fled fast and faster than boat and steam-car, and yet must ever impatiently await them; away from the hard-voiced city, away from the flickering sea into my own Berkshire Hills that sit all sadly guarding the gates of Massachusetts.

Up the stairs I ran to the wan mother and whimpering babe, to the sanctuary on whose altar a life at my bidding had offered itself to win a life, and won. What is this tiny formless thing, this newborn wail from an unknown world, — all head and voice? I handle it curiously, and watch perplexed its winking, breathing, and sneezing. I did not love it then; it seemed a ludicrous thing to love; but her I loved, my girl-mother, she whom now I saw unfolding like the glory of the morning — the transfigured woman. Through her I came to love the wee thing, as it grew strong; as its little soul unfolded itself in twitter and cry and half-formed word, and as its eyes caught the gleam and flash of life. How beautiful he was, with his olive-tinted flesh and dark gold ringlets, his eyes of mingled blue and brown, his perfect little limbs, and the soft voluptuous roll which the blood of Africa had moulded into his features! I held him in my arms, after we had sped far away to our Southern home, — held him, and glanced at the hot red soil of Georgia and the breathless city of a hundred hills, and felt a vague unrest. Why was his hair tinted with gold? An evil omen was golden hair in my life. Why had not the brown of his eyes crushed out and killed the blue? — for brown were his father's eyes, and his father's father's. And thus in the Land of the Color-line I saw, as it fell across my baby, the shadow of the Veil.

Within the Veil was he born, said I; and there within shall he live, — a Negro and a Negro's son. Holding in that little head — ah, bitterly! — the unbowed pride of a hunted race, clinging with that tiny dimpled hand — ah, wearily! — to a hope not hopeless but unhopeful, and seeing with those bright wondering eyes that peer into my soul a land whose freedom is to us a mockery and whose liberty a lie. I saw the shadow of the Veil as it passed over my baby, I saw the cold city towering above the blood-red land. I held my face beside his little cheek, showed him the star-children and the twinkling lights as they began to flash, and stilled with an even-song the unvoiced terror of my life.

So sturdy and masterful he grew, so filled with bubbling life, so tremulous with the unspoken wisdom of a life but eighteen months distant from the All-life, — we were not far from worshipping this revelation of the divine, my wife and I. Her own life builded and moulded itself upon the child; he tinged her every dream and idealized her every effort. No hands but hers must touch and garnish those little limbs; no dress or frill must touch them that had not wearied her fingers; no voice but hers could coax him off to Dreamland, and she and he together spoke some soft and unknown tongue and in it held communion. I too mused above this little white bed; saw the strength of my own arm stretched onward through the ages through the newer strength of his; saw the dream of my black fathers stagger a step onward in the wild phantasm of the world; heard in his baby voice the voice of the Prophet that was to rise within the Veil.

And so we dreamed and loved and planned by fall and winter, and the full flush of the long Southern spring, till the hot winds rolled from the fetid Gulf, till the roses shivered and the still stern sun quivered its awful light over the hills of Atlanta. And then one night the little feet pattered wearily to the wee white bed, and the tiny hands trembled; and a warm flushed face tossed on the pillow, and we knew baby was sick. Ten days he lay there, — a swift week and three endless days, wasting, wasting away. Cheerily the mother nursed him the first days, and laughed into the little eyes that smiled again. Tenderly then she hovered round him, till the smile fled away and Fear crouched beside the little bed.

Then the day ended not, and night was a dreamless terror, and joy and sleep slipped away. I hear now that Voice at midnight calling me from dull and dreamless trance,—crying, "The Shadow of Death! The Shadow of Death!" Out into the starlight I crept, to rouse the gray physician, — the Shadow of Death, the Shadow of Death. The hours trembled on; the night listened; the ghastly dawn glided like a tired thing across the lamplight. Then we two alone looked upon the child as he turned toward us with great eyes, and stretched his stringlike hands, — the Shadow of Death! And we spoke no word, and turned away.

He died at eventide, when the sun lay like a brooding sorrow above the western hills, veiling its face; when the winds spoke not, and the trees, the great green trees he loved, stood motionless. I saw his breath beat quicker and quicker, pause, and then his little soul leapt like a star that travels in the night and left a world of darkness in its train. The day changed not; the same tall trees peeped in at the windows, the same green grass glinted in the setting sun. Only in the chamber of death writhed the world's most piteous thing — a childless mother.

I shirk not. I long for work. I pant for a life full of striving. I am no coward, to shrink before the rugged rush of the storm, nor even quail before the awful shadow of the Veil. But hearken, O Death! Is not this my life hard enough, — is not that dull land that stretches its sneering web about me cold enough, — is not all the world beyond these four little walls pitiless enough, but that thou must needs enter here, — thou, O Death? About my head the thundering storm beat like a heartless voice, and the crazy forest pulsed with the curses of the weak; but what cared I, within my home beside my wife and baby boy? Wast thou so jealous of one little coign of happiness that thou must needs enter there, — thou, O Death?

A perfect life was his, all joy and love, with tears to make it brighter, — sweet as a summer's day beside the Housatonic. The world loved him; the women kissed his curls, the men looked gravely into his wonderful eyes, and the children hovered and fluttered about him. I can see him now, changing like the sky from sparkling laughter to darkening frowns, and then to wondering thoughtfulness as he watched the world. He knew no color-line, poor dear, — and the Veil, though it shadowed him, had not yet darkened half his sun. He loved the white matron, he loved his black nurse; and in his little world walked souls alone, uncolored and unclothed. I — yea, all men — are larger and purer by the infinite breadth of that one little life. She who in simple clearness of vision sees beyond the stars said when he had flown, "He will be happy There; he ever loved beautiful things." And I, far more ignorant, and blind by the web of mine own weaving, sit alone winding words and muttering, "If still he be, and he be There, and there be a There, let him be happy, O Fate!"

Blithe was the morning of his burial, with bird and song and sweet-smelling flowers. The trees whispered to the grass, but the children sat with hushed faces. And yet it seemed a ghostly unreal day, — the wraith of Life. We seemed to rumble down an unknown street behind a little white bundle of posies, with the shadow of a song in our ears. The busy city dinned about us; they did not say much, those pale-faced hurrying men and women; they did not say much, — they only glanced and said, "Niggers!"

We could not lay him in the ground there in Georgia, for the earth there is strangely red; so we bore him away to the northward, with his flowers and his little folded hands. In vain, in vain! — for where, O God! beneath thy broad blue sky shall my dark baby rest in peace, — where Reverence dwells, and Goodness, and a Freedom that is free?

All that day and all that night there sat an awful gladness in my heart, — nay, blame me not if I see the world thus darkly through the Veil, — and my soul whispers ever to me, saying, "Not dead, not dead, but escaped; not bond, but free." No bitter meanness now shall sicken his baby heart till it die a living death, no taunt shall madden his happy boyhood. Fool that I was to think or wish that this little soul should grow choked and deformed within the Veil! I might have known that yonder deep unworldly look that ever and anon floated past his eyes was peering far beyond this narrow Now. In the poise of his little curl-crowned head did there not sit all that wild pride of being which his father had hardly crushed in his own heart? For what, forsooth, shall a Negro want with pride amid the studied humiliations of fifty million fellows? Well sped, my boy, before the world had dubbed your ambition insolence, had held your ideals unattainable, and taught you to cringe and bow. Better far this nameless void that stops my life than a sea of sorrow for you.

Idle words; he might have borne his burden more bravely than we, — aye, and found it lighter too, some day; for surely, surely this is not the end. Surely there shall yet dawn some mighty morning to lift the Veil and set the prisoned free. Not for me, — I shall die in my bonds, — but for fresh young souls who have not known the night and waken to the morning; a morning when men ask of the workman, not "Is he white?" but "Can he work?" When men ask artists, not "Are they black?" but "Do they know?" Some morning this may be, long, long years to come. But now there wails, on that dark shore within the Veil, the same deep voice, *Thou shalt forego!* And all have I foregone at that command, and with small complaint, — all save that fair young form that lies so coldly wed with death in the nest I had builded.

If one must have gone, why not I? Why may I not rest me from this restlessness and sleep from this wide waking? Was not the world's alembic, Time, in his young hands, and is not my time warning? Are there so many workers in the vineyard that the fair promise of this little body could lightly be tossed away? The wretched of my race that line the alleys of the nation sit fatherless and unmothered; but Love sat beside his cradle, and in his ear Wisdom waited to speak. Perhaps now he knows the All-love, and needs not to be wise. Sleep, then, child, — sleep till I sleep and waken to a baby voice and the ceaseless patter of little feet — above the Veil.

In the following selection, W. E. B. DuBois paid eloquent tribute to Alexander Crummell, whose achievements are represented earlier in this book.

Of Alexander Crummell

Then from the Dawn it seemed there came, but faint
As from beyond the limit of the world,
Like the last echo born of a great cry,
Sounds, as if some fair city were one voice
Around a king returning from his wars.

TENNYSON.

This is the history of a human heart, — the tale of a black boy
who many long years ago began to struggle with life that he
might know the world and know himself. Three temptations he
met on those dark dunes that lay gray and dismal before the
wonder-eyes of the child: the temptation of Hate, that stood out
against the red dawn; the temptation of Despair, that darkened
noonday; and the temptation of Doubt, that ever steals along
with twilight. Above all, you must hear of the vales he crossed,
— the Valley of Humiliation and the Valley of the Shadow of
Death.

I saw Alexander Crummell first at a Wilberforce commence-
ment season, amid its bustle and crush. Tall, frail, and black he
stood, with simple dignity and an unmistakable air of good breed-
ing. I talked with him apart, where the storming of the lusty
young orators could not harm us. I spoke to him politely, then
curiously, then eagerly, as I began to feel the fineness of his
character, — his calm courtesy, the sweetness of his strength, and
his fair blending of the hope and truth of life. Instinctively I
bowed before this man, as one bows before the prophets of the
world. Some seer he seemed, that came not from the crimson
Past or the gray To-come, but from the pulsing Now, — that
mocking world which seemed to me at once so light and dark, so
splendid and sordid. Four-score years had he wandered in this
same world of mine, within the Veil.

He was born with the Missouri Compromise and lay a-dying amid the echoes of Manila and El Caney: stirring times for living, times dark to look back upon, darker to look forward to. The black-faced lad that paused over his mud and marbles seventy years ago saw puzzling vistas as he looked down the world. The slave-ship still groaned across the Atlantic, faint cries burdened the Southern breeze, and the great black father whispered mad tales of cruelty into those young ears. From the low doorway the mother silently watched her boy at play, and at nightfall sought him eagerly lest the shadows bear him away to the land of slaves.

So his young mind worked and winced and shaped curiously a vision of Life; and in the midst of that vision ever stood one dark figure alone, — ever with the hard, thick countenance of that bitter father, and a form that fell in vast and shapeless folds. Thus the temptation of Hate grew and shadowed the growing child, — gliding stealthily into his laughter, fading into his play, and seizing his dreams by day and night with rough, rude turbulence. So the black boy asked of sky and sun and flower the never-answered Why? and loved, as he grew, neither the world nor the world's rough ways.

Strange temptation for a child, you may think; and yet in this wide land to-day a thousand thousand dark children brood before this same temptation, and feel its cold and shuddering arms. For them, perhaps, some one will some day lift the Veil, — will come tenderly and cheerily into those sad little lives and brush the brooding hate away, just as Beriah Green strode in upon the life of Alexander Crummell. And before the bluff, kind-hearted man the shadow seemed less dark. Beriah Green had a school in Oneida County, New York, with a score of mischievous boys. "I'm going to bring a black boy here to educate," said Beriah Green, as only a crank and an abolitionist would have dared to say. "Oho!" laughed the boys. "Ye-es," said his wife; and Alexander came. Once before, the black boy had sought a school, had travelled, cold and hungry, four hundred miles up into free New Hampshire, to Canaan. But the godly farmers hitched ninety yoke of oxen to the abolition schoolhouse and dragged it into the middle of the swamp. The black boy trudged away.

The nineteenth was the first century of human sympathy, — the age when half wonderingly we began to descry in others that transfigured spark of divinity which we call Myself; when clod-hoppers and peasants, and tramps and thieves, and millionaires and — sometimes — Negroes, became throbbing souls whose warm pulsing life touched us so nearly that we half gasped with surprise, crying, "Thou too! Hast Thou seen Sorrow and the dull waters of Hopelessness? Hast Thou known Life?" And then all helplessly we peered into those Other-worlds, and wailed, "O World of Worlds, how shall man make you one?"

So in that little Oneida school there came to those schoolboys a revelation of thought and longing beneath one black skin, of which they had not dreamed before. And to the lonely boy came a new dawn of sympathy and inspiration. The shadowy, formless thing — the temptation of Hate, that hovered between him and the world — grew fainter and less sinister. It did not wholly fade away, but diffused itself and lingered thick at the edges. Through it the child now first saw the blue and gold of life, — the sun-swept road that ran 'twixt heaven and earth until in one far-off wan wavering line they met and kissed. A vision of life came to the growing boy,—mystic, wonderful. He raised his head, stretched himself, breathed deep of the fresh new air. Yonder, behind the forests, he heard strange sounds; then glinting through the trees he saw, far, far away, the bronzed hosts of a nation calling, — calling faintly, calling loudly. He heard the hateful clank of their chains; he felt them cringe and grovel, and there rose within him a protest and a prophecy. And he girded himself to walk down the world.

A voice and vision called him to be a priest, — a seer to lead the uncalled out of the house of bondage. He saw the headless host turn toward him like the whirling of mad waters, — he stretched forth his hands eagerly, and then, even as he stretched them, suddenly there swept across the vision the temptation of Despair.

They were not wicked men, — the problem of life is not the problem of the wicked, — they were calm, good men, Bishops of the Apostolic Church of God, and strove toward righteousness. They said slowly, "It is all very natural—it is even commendable; but the General Theological Seminary of the Episcopal Church cannot admit a Negro." And when that thin, half-grotesque figure still haunted their doors, they put their hands kindly, half sorrowfully, on his shoulders, and said, "Now, — of course, we — we know how *you* feel about it; but you see it is impossible, — that is — well — it is premature. Sometime, we trust — sincerely trust — all such distinctions will fade away; but now the world is as it is."

This was the temptation of Despair; and the young man fought it doggedly. Like some grave shadow he flitted by those halls, pleading, arguing, half angrily demanding admittance, until there came the final *No:* until men hustled the disturber away, marked him as foolish, unreasonable, and injudicious, a vain rebel against God's law. And then from that Vision Splendid all the glory faded slowly away, and left an earth gray and stern rolling on beneath a dark despair. Even the kind hands that stretched themselves toward him from out the depths of that dull morning seemed but parts of the purple shadows. He saw them coldly, and asked, "Why should I strive by special grace when the way of the world is closed to me?" All gently yet, the hands urged him on, — the hands of young John Jay, that daring father's daring son; the hands of the good folk of Boston, that free city. And yet, with a way to the priesthood of the Church open at least before him, the cloud lingered there; and even when in old St. Paul's the venerable Bishop raised his white arms above the Negro deacon — even then the burden had not lifted from that heart, for there had passed a glory from the earth.

And yet the fire through which Alexander Crummell went did not burn in vain. Slowly and more soberly he took up again his plan of life. More critically he studied the situation. Deep down below the slavery and servitude of the Negro' people he saw their fatal weaknesses, which long years of mistreatment had emphasized. The dearth of strong moral character, of unbending righteousness, he felt, was their great shortcoming, and here he would begin. He would gather the best of his people into some little Episcopal chapel and there lead, teach, and inspire them, till the leaven spread, till the children grew, till the world hearkened, till — till — and then across his dream gleamed some faint after-glow of that first fair vision of youth — only an after-glow, for there had passed a glory from the earth.

One day — it was in 1842, and the springtide was struggling merrily with the May winds of New England — he stood at last in his own chapel in Providence, a priest of the Church. The days sped by, and the dark young clergyman labored; he wrote his sermons carefully; he intoned his prayers with a soft, earnest voice; he haunted the streets and accosted the wayfarers; he visited the sick, and knelt beside the dying. He worked and toiled, week by week, day by day, month by month. And yet month by month the congregation dwindled, week by week the hollow walls echoed more sharply, day by day the calls came fewer and fewer, and day by day the third temptation sat clearer and still more clearly within the Veil; a temptation, as it were, bland and smiling, with just a shade of mockery in its smooth tones. First it came casually, in the cadence of a voice: "Oh, colored folks? Yes." Or perhaps more definitely: "What do you *expect?*" In voice and gesture lay the doubt — the temptation of Doubt. How he hated it, and stormed at it furiously! "Of course they are capable," he cried; "of course they can learn and strive and achieve — " and "Of course," added the temptation softly, "they do nothing of the sort." Of all the three temptations, this one struck the deepest. Hate? He had outgrown so childish a thing. Despair? He had steeled his right arm against it, and fought it with the vigor of determination. But to doubt the worth of his life-work, — to doubt the destiny and capability of the race his soul loved because it was his; to find listless squalor instead of eager endeavor; to hear his own lips whispering, "They do not care; they cannot know; they are dumb driven cattle, — why cast your pearls before swine?" — this, this seemed more than man could bear; and he closed the door, and sank upon the steps of the chancel, and cast his robe upon the floor and writhed.

The evening sunbeams had set the dust to dancing in the gloomy chapel when he arose. He folded his vestments, put away the hymn-books, and closed the great Bible. He stepped out into the twilight, looked back upon the narrow little pulpit with a weary smile, and locked the door. Then he walked briskly to the Bishop, and told the Bishop what the Bishop already knew. "I have failed," he said simply. And gaining courage by the confession, he added: "What I need is a large constituency. There are comparatively few Negroes here, and perhaps they are not of the best. I must go where the field is wider, and try again." So the Bishop sent him to Philadelphia, with a letter to Bishop Onderdonk.

Bishop Onderdonk lived at the head of six white steps, — corpulent, red-faced, and the author of several thrilling tracts on Apostolic Succession. It was after dinner, and the Bishop had settled himself for a pleasant season of contemplation, when the bell must needs ring, and there must burst in upon the Bishop a letter and a thin, ungainly Negro. Bishop Onderdonk read the letter hastily and frowned. Fortunately, his mind was already clear on this point; and he cleared his brow and looked at Crummell. Then he said, slowly and impressively: "I will receive you into this diocese on one condition: no Negro priest can sit in my church convention, and no Negro church must ask for representation there."

I sometimes fancy I can see that tableau: the frail black figure, nervously twitching his hat before the massive abdomen of Bishop Onderdonk; his threadbare coat thrown against the dark woodwork of the bookcases, where Fox's "Lives of the Martyrs" nested happily beside "The Whole Duty of Man." I seem to see the wide eyes of the Negro wander past the Bishop's broadcloth to where the swinging glass doors of the cabinet glow in the sunlight. A little blue fly is trying to cross the yawning keyhole. He marches briskly up to it, peers into the chasm in a surprised sort of way, and rubs his feelers reflectively; then he essays its depths, and, finding it bottomless, draws back again. The dark-faced priest finds himself wondering if the fly too has faced its Valley of Humiliation, and if it will plunge into it, — when lo! it spreads its tiny wings and buzzes merrily across, leaving the watcher wingless and alone.

Then the full weight of his burden fell upon him. The rich walls wheeled away, and before him lay the cold rough moor winding on through life, cut in twain by one thick granite ridge, — here, the Valley of Humiliation; yonder, the Valley of the Shadow of Death. And I know not which be darker, — no, not I. But this I know: in yonder Vale of the Humble stand to-day a million swarthy men, who willingly would

> ". . . bear the whips and scorns of time,
> The oppressor's wrong, the proud man's contumely,
> The pangs of despised love, the law's delay,
> The insolence of office, and the spurns
> That patient merit of the unworthy takes,"—

all this and more would they bear did they but know that this were sacrifice and not a meaner thing. So surged the thought within that lone black breast. The Bishop cleared his throat suggestively; then, recollecting that there was really nothing to say, considerately said nothing, only sat tapping his foot impatiently. But Alexander Crummell said, slowly and heavily: "I will never enter your diocese on such terms." And saying this, he turned and passed into the Valley of the Shadow of Death. You might have noted only the physical dying, the shattered frame and hacking cough; but in that soul lay deeper death than that. He found a chapel in New York, — the church of his father; he labored for it in poverty and starvation, scorned by his fellow priests. Half in despair, he wandered across the sea, a beggar with outstretched hands. Englishmen clasped them, — Wilberforce and Stanley, Thirwell and Ingles, and even Froude and Macaulay; Sir Benjamin Brodie bade him rest awhile at Queen's College in Cambridge, and there he lingered, struggling for health of body and mind, until he took his degree in '53. Restless still and unsatisfied, he turned toward Africa, and for long years, amid the spawn of the slave-smugglers, sought a new heaven and a new earth.

So the man groped for light; all this was not Life, — it was the world-wandering of a soul in search of itself, the striving of one who vainly sought his place in the world, ever haunted by the shadow of a death that is more than death, — the passing of a soul that has missed its duty. Twenty years he wandered, — twenty years and more; and yet the hard rasping question kept gnawing within him, "What, in God's name, am I on earth for?" In the narrow New York parish his soul seemed cramped and smothered. In the fine old air of the English University he heard the millions wailing over the sea. In the wild fever-cursed swamps of West Africa he stood helpless and alone.

You will not wonder at his weird pilgrimage, — you who in the swift whirl of living, amid its cold paradox and marvellous vision, have fronted life and asked its riddle face to face. And if you find that riddle hard to read, remember that yonder black boy finds it just a little harder; if it is difficult for you to find and face your duty, it is a shade more difficult for him; if your heart sickens in the blood and dust of battle, remember that to him the dust is thicker and the battle fiercer. No wonder the wanderers fall! No wonder we point to thief and murderer, and haunting prostitute, and the never-ending throng of unhearsed dead! The Valley of the Shadow of Death gives few of its pilgrims back to the world.

But Alexander Crummell it gave back. Out of the temptation of Hate, and burned by the fire of Despair, triumphant over Doubt, and steeled by Sacrifice against Humiliation, he turned at last home across the waters, humble and strong, gentle and determined. He bent to all the gibes and prejudices, to all hatred and discrimination, with that rare courtesy which is the armor of pure souls. He fought among his own, the low, the grasping, and the wicked, with that unbending righteousness which is the sword of the just. He never faltered, he seldom complained; he simply worked, inspiring the young, rebuking the old, helping the weak, guiding the strong.

So he grew, and brought within his wide influence all that was best of those who walk within the Veil. They who live without knew not nor dreamed of that full power within, that mighty inspiration which the dull gauze of caste decreed that most men should not know. And now that he is gone, I sweep the Veil away and cry, Lo! the soul to whose dear memory I bring this little tribute. I can see his face still, dark and heavy lined beneath his snowy hair; lighting and shading, now with inspiration for the future, now in innocent pain at some human wickedness, now with sorrow at some hard memory from the past. The more I met Alexander Crummell, the more I felt how much that world was losing which knew so little of him. In another age he might have sat among the elders of the land in purple-bordered toga; in another country mothers might have sung him to the cradles.

He did his work, — he did it nobly and well; and yet I sorrow that here he worked alone, with so little human sympathy. His name to-day, in this broad land, means little, and comes to fifty million ears laden with no incense of memory or emulation. And herein lies the tragedy of the age: not that men are poor, — all men know something of poverty; not that men are wicked, — who is good? not that men are ignorant, — what is Truth? Nay, but that men know so little of men.

He sat one morning gazing toward the sea. He smiled and said, "The gate is rusty on the hinges." That night at star-rise a wind came moaning out of the west to blow the gate ajar, and then the soul I loved fled like a flame across the Seas, and in its seat sat Death.

I wonder where he is to-day? I wonder if in that dim world beyond, as he came gliding in, there rose on some wan throne a King, — a dark and pierced Jew, who knows the writhings of the earthly damned, saying, as he laid those heart-wrung talents down, "Well done!" while round about the morning stars sat singing.

Kelly Miller (1863-1939)

Frederick Douglass

For a generation, Kelly Miller was an intellectual champion of Negro Americans. Born in Winnsboro, South Carolina, he was educated at Howard University and at Johns Hopkins (A.M., 1901; LL.D 1903). He was a member of the faculty of Howard University, where he taught mathematics and sociology and served as dean of the College of Arts and Sciences. A frequent lecturer and essayist on controversial subjects, he collected his writings in *Race Adjustment* (1908), *Out of the House of Bondage* (1914), *An Appeal to Conscience* (1918), *History of the World War and the Important Part Taken by the Negroes* (1919), and *The Everlasting Stain* (1924).

The following selection is not in Miller's most characteristic vein of defense or attack. Instead, in an essay which is a model for organization and direct presentation of an idea, Miller explains the significance of Frederick Douglass, whose work is represented earlier in this book.

Frederick Douglass

The highest function of a great name is to serve as an example and as a perpetual source of inspiration to the young who are to come after him. By the subtle law known as "consciousness of

From *Race Adjustment*: *Essays on the Negro in America*. (New York: Neale, 1908).

kind" a commanding personality incites the sharpest stimulus and exerts the deepest intensity of influence among the group from which he springs. We gather inspiration most readily from those of our class who have been touched with the feeling of our infirmities and have been subject to like conditions as ourselves. Every class, every race, every country, and indeed every well-defined group of social interests has its own glorified names whose fame and following are limited to the prescribed sphere of influence. Indeed, human relations are so diverse and human interests and feelings so antagonistic that the names which command even a fanatical following among one class may be despised and rejected by another. He who serves his exclusive class may be great in the positive degree; the man who serves a whole race or country may be considered great in the comparative degree; but it is only the man who breaks the barrier of class and creed and country and serves the human race that is worthy to be accounted great in the superlative degree. We are so far the creatures of local and institutional environment, and so disposed to borrow our modes of thought and feeling from our social medium, that even an appeal to the universal heart must be adapted to the spirit and genius of the time and people to whom it is first made. Even the Saviour of the world offered the plan of salvation first to the Jews in the traditional guise of the Hebrew cult.

It is essential that any isolated, proscribed class should honor its illustrious names. They serve not only as a measure of their possibilities, but they possess greater inspirational power by virtue of their close sympathetic and kindly touch. Small wonder that such people are wont to glorify their distinguished men out of proportion to their true historical setting on the scale of human greatness.

Frederick Douglass is the one commanding historic character of the colored race in America. He is the model of emulation of those who are struggling up through the trials and difficulties which he himself suffered and subdued. He is illustrative and exemplary of what they might become — the first fruit of promise of a dormant race. To the aspiring colored youth of this land Mr. Douglass is, at once, the inspiration of their hopes and the justification of their claims.

I do not on this occasion intend to dwell upon the well-known facts and circumstances in the life and career of Mr. Douglass, but deem it more profitable to point out some of the lessons to be derived from that life.

In the first place, Mr. Douglass began life at the lowest possible level. It is only when we understand the personal circumstances of his early environment that we can appreciate the pathos and power with which he was wont to insist upon the true measure of the progress of the American Negro, not by the height already attained, but by the depth from which he came. It has been truly said that it required a greater upward move to bring Mr. Douglass to the status in which the ordinary white child is born than is necessary on the part of the latter to reach the presidency of the United States. The early life of this gifted child of nature was spent amid squalor, deprivation and cruel usage. Like Melchizedek of old, it can be said of him that he sprang into existence without father or mother, or beginning of days. His little body was unprotected from the bitter, biting cold, and his vitals griped with the gnawing pangs of hunger. We are told that he vied with the dogs for the crumbs that fell from his master's table. He tasted the sting of a cruel slavery, and drank the cup to its very dregs. And yet he arose from this lowly and degraded estate and gained for himself a place among the illustrious names of his country.

We hear much in this day and time about the relative force of environment and heredity as factors in the formation of character. But, as the career of Mr. Douglass illustrates, there is a subtle power of personality which, though the product of neither, is more potential than both. God has given to each of us an irrepressible inner something, which, for want of better designation, the old philosophy used to call the freedom of the will, which counts for most in the making of manhood.

In the second place, I would call attention to the tremendous significance of a seemingly trifling incident in his life. When he was about thirteen years of age he came into possession of a copy of the "Columbian Orator," abounding in dramatic outbursts and stirring episodes of liberty. It was the ripened fruit of the choicest spirits, upon which the choicest spirits feed. This book fired his whole soul and kindled an unquenchable love for liberty. It is held by some that at the age of puberty the mind is in a state of unstable equilibrium, and, like a pyramid on its apex, may be thrown in any direction by the slightest impression of force. The instantaneity of religious conversions, which the Methodists used to acclaim with such triumphant outbursts of hallelujah, may rest upon some such psychological foundation. When the child nature stands at the parting of the ways, between youth and adolescence, it yields to some quickening touch, as the fuse to the spark, or as the sensitized plate to the impressions of sunlight. There are "psychological moments" when the revealed idea rises sublimely above the revealing agent. According to the theory of harmonies, if two instruments are tuned in resonant accord the vibrations of the one will wake up the slumbering chords of the other. Young Douglass's soul was in sympathetic resonance with the great truth of human brotherhood and equality, and needed only the psychological suggestion which the "Columbian Orator" supplied. In a moment, in the twinkling of an eye, it burned deep into his soul and made an ineffaceable impression upon his consciousness of the gospel of brotherhood and equality of man. It was the same truth which could only be impressed upon the Apostle Peter in the rhapsodies of a heavenly vision. The age of revelation is not past, and will not pass so long as there remains one soul that yearns for spiritual illumination. There comes at times into our lives some sudden echo of the heavenly harmony from the unseen world, and happy is that soul which beats in vibrant harmony with that supernal sound. When the gospel of liberty first dawned upon the adolescent Douglass, as he perused the pages of the "Columbian Orator," there is no rendition of either the old or the new school of psychology that can analyze the riot of thought and sentiment that swept through his turbulent soul. This was indeed his new birth, his baptism with fire from on high. From that moment he was a possessed man. The love of liberty bound him with its subtle cords and did not release him until the hour of his death on Anacostia's mist-clad height.

Our educational philosophers are ransacking their brains to prescribe wise curricula of study for colored youth. There is not so much need of that which gives information to the mind or cunning to the fingers as that which touches the soul and quickens the spirit. There must be first aroused dormant consciousness of manhood with its inalienable rights, privileges, and dignity. The letter killeth, the spirit maketh alive. The "Columbian Orator" contributed more toward arousing the manhood of Mr. Douglass than all the traditional knowledge of all the schools. Of what avail is the mastery of all branches of technical and refined knowledge unless it touches the hidden springs of manhood? The value of any curriculum of study for a suppressed class that is not pregnant with moral energy, and that does not make insistent and incessant appeal to the half-conscious manhood within is seriously questionable. The revelation to a young man of the dignity, I had almost said the divinity, of his own selfhood is worth more to him in the development of character and power than all the knowledge in all the de luxe volumes in the gilded Carnegie libraries.

In the third place, Negro youth should study Mr. Douglass as a model of manly courage. In order to acquire a clear conception of principles let us discriminate sharply in the use of terms. Courage is that quality which enables one to encounter danger and difficulties with firmness and resolution of spirit. It is the swell of soul which meets outward pressure with inner resistance. Fortitude, on the other hand, is the capacity to endure, the ability to suffer and be strong. It is courage in the passive voice. True courage sets up an ideal and posits a purpose; it calculates the cost and is economic of means, though never faltering in determination to reach that end. Bravery is mere physical daring in the presence of danger, and responds to temporary physical and mental excitation. He who is eager to fight every evil which God allows to exist in society does not display rational courage. Even our Saviour selected the evils against which He waged war. The caged eagle which beats his wings into insensibility against the iron bars of his prison-house is accounted a foolish bird. On the other hand, "the linnet void of noble raze" has gained the everlasting seal of poetic disapproval. It is not genuine courage to go through the world like the knight in the tale with sword in hand and challenge on lips to offer mortal combat to every windmill of opposition.

Mr. Douglass was courageous in the broadest and best significance of the term. He set before him as the goal of his ambition his own personal freedom and that of his race, and he permitted neither principalities nor powers, nor height nor depth, nor things present nor things to come, to swerve him from the pursuit of that purpose.

When we speak of moral courage we indulge in tautology of terms; for all courage is essentially moral. It does not require courage to go with your friends or against your enemies; it is a physical impulse to do so. But true moral courage is shown when we say no to our friends.

Mr. Douglass reached the climax of moral courage when he parted with William Lloyd Garrison, his friend and benefactor, because of honest difference of judgment, and when for the same motive he refused to follow John Brown to the scaffold at Harper's Ferry. It required an iron resolution and sublime courage for

Douglass to deny the tender, pathetic, paternal appeal of the man who was about to offer up himself as a sacrifice for an alien race. John Brown on the scaffold dying for an alien and defenseless race is the most sublime spectacle that this planet has seen since Christ hung on the cross. That scaffold shall be more hallowed during the ages to come than any throne upon which king ever sat. Who but Douglass would decline a seat on his right hand?

In the fourth place, Mr. Douglass stands out as a model of self-respect. Although he was subject to all of the degradation and humiliation of his race, yet he preserved the integrity of his own soul. It is natural for a class that is despised, rejected and despitefully used to accept the estimate of their contemners, and to conclude that they are good for nothing but to be cast out and trodden under foot. In a civilization whose every feature serves to impress a whole people with a sense of their inferiority, small wonder if the more timid and resigned spirits are crushed beneath the cruel weight. It requires the philosophic calm and poise to stand upright and unperturbed amid such irrational things.

It is imperative that the youth of the colored race have impressed upon them the lesson that it is not the treatment that a man receives that degrades him, but that which he accepts. It does not degrade the soul when the body is swallowed up by the earthquake or overwhelmed by the flood. We are not humiliated by the rebuffs of nature. No more should we feel humiliated and degraded by violence and outrage perpetrated by a powerful and arrogant social scheme. As a man thinketh in his heart, so is he. The inner freedom of soul is not subject to assault and battery. Mr. Douglass understood this principle well. He was never in truth and in deed a slave; for his soul never accepted the gyves that shackled his body.

It is related that Mr. Douglass was once ordered out of a first-class coach into a "Jim Crow" car by a rude and ill-mannered conductor. His white companion followed him to the prescribed department, and asked him how he felt to be humiliated by such a coarse fellow. Mr. Douglass let himself out to the full length of his robust manhood and replied, "I feel as if I had been kicked by an ass." If one will preserve his inner integrity, the ill-usage and despiteful treatment others may heap upon him can never penetrate to the holy of holies, which remains sacred and inviolable to an external assault.

The fifth lesson which should be emphasized in connection with the life of Mr. Douglass is that he possessed a ruling passion outside the narrow circle of self-interest and personal well being. The love of liberty reigned supreme in his soul. All great natures are characterized by a passionate enthusiasm for some altruistic principle. Its highest manifestation is found in the zeal for the salvation of men on the spiritual side. All great religious teachers belong to this class. Patriots and philanthropists are ardently devoted to the present well-being of man. The poet, the painter, and the sculptor indulge in a fine frenzy over contemplative beauty or its formal expression. The philosopher and the scientist go into ecstasy over the abstract pursuit of truth. Minds of smaller caliber get pure delight from empty pleasure, sportsmanship or the collection of curios and bric-à-brac. Even the average man is at his highest level when his whole soul goes out in love for another. The man who lives without altruistic enthusiasm goes through the world wrapped in a shroud.

There have been few members of the human race that have been characterized by so intense and passionate a love for liberty as Frederick Douglass. His love for liberty was not limited by racial, political or geographical boundaries, but included the whole round world. He believed that liberty, like religion, applied to all men "without one plea." He championed liberty for black men, liberty for white men, liberty for Americans, liberty for Europeans, liberty for Asiatics, liberty for the wise, liberty for the simple; liberty for the weak, liberty for the strong; liberty for men, liberty for women; liberty for all the sons and daughters of men. I do not know whether he permitted his thoughts to wander in planetary space or speculated as to the inhabitability of other worlds than ours; but if he did, I am sure that his great soul took them all in his comprehensive scheme of liberty. In this day and time, when the spirit of commercialism and selfish greed command the best energies of the age, the influence of such a life to those who are downtrodden and overborne is doubly significant Greed for gain has never righted any wrong in the history of the human race. The love of money is the root, and not the remedy of evil.

In the sixth and last place, I would call attention of the young to the danger of forgetting the work and worth of Frederick Douglass and the ministrations of his life. We live in a practical age when the things that are seen overshadow the things that are invisible.

What did Douglass do? ask the crass materialists. He built no institutions and laid no material foundations. True, he left us no showy tabernacles of clay. He did not aspire to be the mechanic of the colored race. The greatest things of this world are not made with hands, but reside in truth and righteousness and love. Douglass was the moral leader and spiritual prophet of his race. Unless all signs of the times are misleading, the time approaches, and is even now at hand, which demands a moral renaissance. Then, O for a Douglass, to arouse the conscience of the white race, to awaken the almost incomprehensible lethargy of his own people, and to call down the righteous wrath of Heaven upon injustice and wrong.

James Weldon Johnson (1871-1938)

Detroit

A man of many talents, James Weldon Johnson at various times was a school teacher, a principal, a lawyer, a leading song writer, a poet, a novelist, a consul for the United States, secretary for the National Association for the Advancement of Colored People, and a college professor. Born in Jacksonville, Florida, he received a Bachelor's degree from Atlanta University. After passing the Florida bar examinations, Johnson, a high-school principal, abandoned both law and education to join his brother Rosamond in New York, where, for several years, the two collaborated in writing successful musical comedies presented on Broadway. From 1906 to 1913 he served as Consul in Venezuela and Nicaragua. After leaving government service, he worked first as field secretary, then as general secretary, for the NAACP from 1916 to 1930. While teaching at Fisk University, whose faculty he joined in 1930, Johnson was killed in an automobile accident.

Although Johnson is best known to literary historians for his novel, *Autobiography of an Ex-Coloured Man* (1912), for his book of poetic folk sermons, *God's Trombones* (1927), for his cultural and social history of Negroes in New York, *Black Manhattan* (1930), or for *Book of American Negro Poetry*, the first anthology of poetry by black Americans, his position as secretary for the NAACP required him to write extensively on contemporary, political, social, and economic issues. In the following selection, he

From *The Crisis* XXXII (July 1926). Reprinted by permission of publishers of *The Crisis*.

describes the trial of Dr. Henry Sweet, who was charged with murder because, after moving into a white residential neighborhood in Detroit, he defended his home against a mob led by individuals organized to prevent Negroes from living in white neighborhoods. The chief defense attorney for Henry Sweet was Clarence Darrow, one of America's most famous trial lawyers.

Detroit

For eight months the National Office has been steeped in the Sweet case. It has whipped up every energy and drawn upon every recourse to carry the fight through to victory. All of us at the office realized the responsibility involved, and carried the whole matter on our hearts.

But when I entered the Recorder's Court of Detroit on Monday morning, May 3, in the midst of the second trial, I felt myself thrust suddenly, as an individual, into an arena of vital conflict and personally engaged in the struggle. I was at once so gripped by the tense drama being enacted before my eyes that I became a part of the tragedy. And tragedy it was. The atmosphere was tragic. The serried rows of colored faces that packed the courtroom from the rail to the back wall, watching and waiting, were like so many tragic masks. The mild, softspoken boy being tried for murder in the first degree and, for the time, carrying the onus of the other ten defendants, and upon whose fate hung the right of the black man to defend himself in his home, was an extremely tragic figure. The twelve white men sitting over against him, under oath to disregard prejudice and to render a true and just verdict between black and white in a land where race prejudice is far more vital than religion, also became tragic figures. The rugged face of Clarence Darrow, more haggard and lined by the anxious days, with the deep, brooding eyes, heightened the intense effect of the whole.

For a week I listened to testimony and the examination of witnesses. Each day the courtroom on the other side of the rail was packed as tightly as the space would permit. First, the witnesses for the prosecution, most of them members of the police force, evading the truth, distorting the truth, actually lying. And why? Because they were opposed to a Negro moving into a white neighborhood? Not primarily. The policemen who testified felt, even though a man's liberty was at stake, that they had to justify the course which the police had followed in the case. And so policeman after policeman, under oath, testified that on the night of the shooting, the streets around the Sweet house were almost deserted. From their description of the scene the vicinity was like Goldsmith's "Deserted Village". And thus they showed themselves willing to swear away a man's liberty for life in order to save the face of the Police Department. For if it was shown that there was a mob around the Sweet home on that fateful night the Police Department would become responsible for all the consequences, because it allowed that mob to assemble. But it was proven that there was a mob of five hundred persons or more. This was proven by disinterested witnesses for the defense; and the police did nothing to prevent the gathering of that mob. From their own testimony they did not ask a single person what he was doing there or to move away.

The witnesses for the prosecution who were not policemen were admittedly prejudiced against colored people and opposed to their living in white neighborhoods. They were for the most part members of the Waterworks Improvement Association, organized for the purpose of keeping colored people out of white neighborhoods, and home owners in the vicinity in which Dr. Sweet had purchased. And so, like the policemen, they were interested witnesses. They did not have their faces to save but they felt that they had their property to save. One of these witnesses with a Germanic name and the face of a moron, on Mr. Darrow's cross-examination, stated that he and his neighbors were organized to keep "undesirables" out of the neighborhood. He, of course, listed Negroes at the head of the "undesirables". When further pressed by Mr. Darrow he added "Italians". When still further pressed he stated that they did not want anybody but Americans. When Mr. Darrow asked him if he knew that Negroes had been in America for more than three hundred years, longer than any of his ancestors, and that America was discovered by a great Italian, he had no words for answer.

Witnesses for the defense restored my faith in human nature — and not because they were for the defense but because they were telling the truth. The white witnesses for the defense were absolutely without interest. It was plain that they could have no motive for testifying that there was a mob around the Sweet house on that eventful night, except in behalf of truth. And although racial interest might have been imputed to the colored witnesses, nevertheless, because they were speaking the truth they carried conviction. And perhaps more impressive still was the fact that the colored witnesses who testified showed themselves far superior intellectually, culturally and socially, to the white witnesses who were among those opposed to the Sweets moving into their neighborhood.

During all the days of the testimony the court and the crowd listened intently to every word that fell from the lips of the witnesses. The crowd was sensitive, like a barometer, to the ups and downs of the testimony. Whenever Darrow or Chawke scored in their cross-examination a ray of light lit the sea of dark faces, and when the prosecutors won a point sombre tragedy would again settle down.

On Saturday night, May 8, both sides rested.

On Monday morning the attorneys for the defense made the motions for dismissal or a directed verdict and, as was expected, the motions were denied. The argument for the State was then opened by the Assistant Prosecuting Attorney who made a fierce attack upon the Sweets and their motives. He closed by drawing for the jury a picture of the cold, stark body of Leon Breiner, the white man who had been killed. He stressed the words, "I hold a brief for Leon Breiner". He was followed in the afternoon by Mr. Chawke for the Defense. Mr. Chawke spoke with all of the skill and power of the great criminal lawyer that he is.

On Tuesday morning every available space in the courtroom was taken up. Even within the railing spectators were closely packed together. There were hundreds of colored people and a large number of interested whites. There were prominent lawyers and jurists of Detroit. When the court opened not another person could be squeezed into the courtroom. Clarence Darrow was to speak.

For nearly seven hours he talked to the jury. I sat where I could catch every word and every expression of his face. It was the most wonderful flow of words I ever heard from a man's lips. Clarence Darrow, the veteran criminal lawyer, the psychologist, the philosopher, the great humanist, the great apostle of liberty, was bringing into play every bit of skill, drawing upon all the knowledge, and using every power that he possessed. Court and jury and spectators had unrolled before them a complete panorama of the experiences, physical and spiritual, of the American Negro, beginning with his African background, down to the present — a panorama of his sufferings, his struggles, his achievements, his aspirations. Mr. Darrow's argument was at once an appeal for the Negro because of the injustice he has suffered, a tribute to him for what he has achieved in spite of handicaps and obstacles, and an indictment of the morality and civilization of America because of the hypocrisies and brutalities of race prejudice. At times his voice was as low as though he were coaxing a reluctant child. At such times the strain upon the listeners to catch his words made them appear almost rigid. At other times his words came like flashes of lightning and crashes of thunder. He closed his agrument with an appeal that did not leave a dry eye in the courtroom. When he finished I walked over to him to express in behalf of the National Association for the Advancement of Colored People my appreciation and thanks. His eyes were shining and wet. He placed his hands on my shoulders. I stammered out a few words but broke down and wept, and I was not ashamed of my tears.

On the following morning the Prosecutor closed the argument for the State. He began as though he intended to rival Mr. Darrow in paying a tribute to the Negro race, but his beginning was only a background to set off what he really meant to say. Some of the things he said brought quick and firm objections from our lawyers. He spoke in rather high terms of the National Association for the Advancement of Colored People and then added that if he had a mind like some people he would say it was an organization for the purpose of foistering colored people into white neighborhoods, for the purpose of promoting social equality, and for the purpose of bringing about an amalgamation of the races. The defense attorneys objected and the Judge admonished, but this appeal to prejudice the jury had already heard. At another time he virtually asked the jury what would they as twelve white men, if they brought in a verdict of not guilty, answer to white men who asked them about their verdict. Here again the defense lawyers objected, but the jury again had heard. In his zeal to convict, the Prosecutor overstepped legal lines and called the jury's attention to the fact that the defendant had not taken the stand and testified in his own behalf to contradict certain statements which had been made. Mr. Chawke was immediately on his feet and objected. The objection was sustained and the grounds were laid for a reversible error. The point was one which has been several times sustained by the Supreme Court of Michigan and the courts of various other states. When the Prosecutor finished the court adjourned for the day.

The next morning, Thursday, the courtroom was again crowded, to hear the charge of the Judge. For two and a half hours Judge Murphy charged the jury. The charge contemplated the law

involved from every point and yet it was not the dry dust of the
law books. It was eloquent and moving. In his charge, as in presiding over the case, Judge Murphy showed himself absolutely fair
and impartial. Indeed, he was in the highest degree the just judge.
The jury went into deliberation immediately after lunch. We were
hopeful but not sanguine. We counted that the worst we could get
would be another mistrial. It was commonly expressed that a
mistrial was the probable verdict. We were heartened by the
fact that, in case of a verdict of guilty in any degree, we held in
our hands the ace of a reversible error.

   I left the courtroom after the charge to the jury and sent a
telegram to the National Office. I walked over to Judge Jayne's
court and talked with him for a while. Then, feeling not at all
like eating, I went back to the courtroom to wait. The crowd that
had waited patiently for days was still waiting. Suddenly there
was a pounding on the jury room door. The officer in charge of the
jury answered and found that the jury wanted further instructions. Neither the Judge nor the attorneys had yet returned from
lunch. There was nothing to indicate the need of hurry. Everybody expected the jury would ask for further instructions and be
locked up for the night. A little later the Judge and the attorneys
returned to the court. The attorneys began to draft instructions
that would be acceptable to both sides on the point raised by the
jury. I sat in the Judge's ante-chamber and watched them while
they worked. Mr. Chawke made the first draft on a yellow pad.
The Prosecuting Attorney revised and amended. Mr. Darrow and
the Assistant Prosecuting Attorney expressed their views. The
draft was at last agreed upon by the four attorneys. The Prosecutor had just torn from the pad the sheets that contained the
written words to pass them in to the Judge when the officer in
charge of the jury entered the room and announced that a verdict
had been reached. Everybody in the room was amazed. We for the
defense, in spite of ourselves, were seized with apprehension. The
probabilities were that a verdict so quickly reached was a compromise verdict. There was even the possibility of a verdict of guilty
as charged. These thoughts ran through all our minds. They
showed themselves in the quickly changing expressions of the
Prosecutors. Both attorneys for the prosecution, perhaps unconsciously, assumed a magnanimous air. It was as much as to say,
"We are sorry; it is too bad; but we had to do our official duty".
These thoughts were quickly transmitted to the waiting crowd in

the courtroom and with the crowd the fears and apprehensions were magnified.

The court re-convened. The judge ascended to the bench. Mr. Chawke came over and whispered a word of encouragement to Henry Sweet. I sat next to Henry Sweet. I put my hand on his arm and said, "No matter what happens the National Association will stand by you to the end."

The jury was called in. They filed in solemnly and took their places facing the bench. The clerk asked, "Gentlemen, have you arrived at a verdict?" The answer was, "We have". I then began to live the most intense thirty seconds of my whole life. The verdict was pronounced by the foreman in a strong, clear voice which filled the courtroom, "Not Guilty".

The effect is electrical. We are transported in a flash from the depths to the heights. Someone starts to applaud but brings his hands together only once. A simultaneous sigh of relief goes up from the hundreds outside the rail. I look around. Women are sobbing convulsively, and tears are running down the cheeks of men. I get a confused vision of Henry Sweet, Dr. Sweet and his wife shaking hands with the jury and thanking them, shaking hands with Mr. Darrow and Mr. Chawke and thanking them. They are followed by others. It seems that everybody is shaking hands and giving thanks.

The verdict was recorded upon the oath of the jury and thus was reached what we believe to be the end of the most dramatic court trial involving the fundamental rights of the Negro in his whole history in this country.

Langston Hughes (1902-1967)

Fooling Our White Folks

Langston Hughes has been described as the most versatile Negro American writer who ever lived. Born in Joplin, Missouri, reared in Kansas and Ohio, he entered Columbia University in 1922 but dropped out after a year of studying. For several years, he worked his way through Europe and Africa before he returned to America, where he became a part of the Harlem Renaissance. After returning to college to earn an undergraduate degree from Lincoln University (Pa.), Hughes became a professional writer and lecturer.

No other Negro writer has matched the variety of Hughes's achievements. Well-known for his attempts to reproduce "jazz" rhythms and "blues" in poetry, he published nine volumes of poems, two novels, and three collections of stories. Fascinated by theater, he established several all-Negro theatrical companies and wrote several plays. Three of his plays were produced on Broadway, and one — *Mulatto* (1934) — enjoyed the longest continuous run of any play written by a Negro before Lorraine Hansberry. In addition, Hughes wrote the libretto for the musical version of Elmer Rice's *Street Scene*, an opera, stories for children, and two autobiographies. He also translated poetry, edited or co-edited anthologies of folklore and poetry, and publicized the musical and literary achievements of Africans and Afro-Americans. Perhaps his most significant literary achievement lies in the many stories, sketches, and essays about Jesse B. Semple ("Simple").

A migrant from Virginia to Harlem, Simple is a memorable character in American literature. Lacking formal education, but richly endowed with intelligence, wit, and pride, he rejoices in the excitement of living while he simultaneously denounces white men who repress Negroes and middle-class Negroes who attempt to escape their racial identity.

As he continued to write for more than thirty years after the Renaissance ended, Hughes, better than any other writer, kept alive the confidence, the laughter, and the zest for living which had characterized the Harlem writers during that exuberant decade. The following selection is characteristic of the manner in which Hughes frequently satirized subjects which other writers have viewed with serious, often excessively serious, concern.

Fooling Our White Folks

I never was one for pushing the phrase "social equality" to the nth degree. I concur with those persons, white or colored, who wish to reserve the right of inviting whom they choose into the house as friends, or as dinner guests. I do not believe civil rights should encroach on personal privacy or personal associations. But health, wealth, work, the ballot, the armed services, are another matter. Such things should be available to whites and Negroes alike in this American country.

But, because our American whites are stupid in so many ways, racially speaking, and because there are many things in this U.S.A. of ours which Negroes may achieve only by guile, I have great tolerance for persons of color who deliberately set out to fool our white folks. I remember the old slave story of the mistress who would not allow her house servants to have any biscuits. She was so particular on this point that she would cut the biscuits out herself and count them. But the cook went her one better. When the mistress left the kitchen, the cook would trim a narrow rim off every biscuit — with the result that the Negroes had in the end a pan of biscuits, too.

A great many Negroes in America are daily engaged in slyly trimming off the biscuits of race prejudice. Most Negroes feel that bigoted white persons deserve to be cheated and fooled since the way they behave toward us makes no moral sense at all. And many Negroes would be way behind the eight ball had they not devised surreptitious means of escape. For those who are able to do it, passing for white is, of course, the most common means of escaping color handicaps. Every large Negro section has many residents who pass for white by day, but come home to their various Harlems at night. I know dozens of colored whites in downtown offices or shops. But at night they are colored again.

Then there are those Negroes who go white permanently. This is perhaps a more precarious game than occupational passing during work hours only. Some break down under the strain and go native again or go to pieces. But hundreds of others pass blithely into the third and fourth generations — entirely losing their dusky horizons by intermarriage. There is one quite well-known Negro family in the East with an equally well-known brother out West who has been "white" for forty years, and whose children's children are "white" — now, no doubt, beyond recall. A famous Negro educator told me recently of having lost track of one of his most brilliant students, only to be asked to address a large and wealthy congregation in the Midwest and to find as pastor of this church his long lost colored graduate, now the "white" shepherd of a white flock. The educator was delighted at his former student's ministerial success in fooling our white folks.

The consensus of opinion among Negroes seems to be approval of those who can get by with it. Almost all of as know Negroes of light complexion who, during the war, were hustled through their draft boards so fast that they were unwittingly put into white units and did their service entirely without the humiliations of the military color bar. One young Negro of my acquaintance took his basic training in Mississippi in a white unit, lived with the white boys, went to all the local dances and parties, and had a wonderful time without the army or Rankin being any the wiser. He is back now in the Negro college from which the draft took him. The army policy being stupid anyway, all his family and friends applaud his having so thoroughly fooled our white folks in the deep South.

Negroes are even more pleased when persons of *obviously* colored complexion succeed in calling white America's bluff. Those young ladies who, in spite of golden or brown complexions, take foreign names and become Hollywood starlets, delight us. And the men who go to Mexico as colored and come back as Spanish to marry wealthy white debutantes gain a great deal of admiration from the bulk of the Negro race. Negroes feel it is good enough for Nordic debutantes to be thusly fooled. Besides, nothing is too good for those with nerve enough to take it. Anyhow, hasn't the army a strange way of classifying black Puerto Ricans as "white" while quite white American Negroes are put down as "colored"? Simple, our white folks: so why not fool them?

When the Waldorf-Astoria first opened in New York, Negroes were not served in its main dining rooms. In a spirt of fun, a well-known Harlem journalist of definitely colored cast, put on a turban and went into the hotel. He was served with the utmost courtesy. During the war a fine Negro chemist, quite brownskin, applied for a position in a war plant and was given a blank to fill out. He truthfully put down his nationality as American, his race as Negro. He received a letter saying no openings were available, in spite of the fact that every day the firm advertised for chemists. He simply procured another blank. Instead of putting down Negro as his race, he wrote Puerto Rican — and was hired at once. Silly, our white folks!

Some Negroes make sport of them all the time. There is a very dark gentleman in a large Midwestern city where prejudice in public places is rampant, who delights in playing upon white gullibility. Being truly African in complexion, he does not pretend to pass for white. He can't. But since many of the restaurants and theatres are owned or managed by foreign-born Americans, or Jewish Americans, he simply passes for whatever the nationality of the management might be at the time. He will tell a Jewish theatre manager who wishes him to sit in the Negro section, "Do you not know that I am a black Hebrew?" Usually the man will be so taken aback that he will say no more. Such sport this patron enjoys more than the films.

He once went into a Greek restaurant at the edge of the Negro section, but which, nevertheless, had a custom of not serving Negroes. He was told he could not eat therein. He said, "but did you never hear of Socrates? He was a black Greek. Many noble Greeks of old were colored. I am descended from such ancient Greeks. What do you mean, *I*, a black Greek, cannot eat here?" He was served without further ado. Funny, our white folks — even those not yet Americanized! They, too, act right simple sometimes.

In the early days of the war, reading my poems at various U.S.O.'s in the South, one day between Nashville and Chattanooga I went into the buffet section of a parlor car coach for luncheon. The Filipino steward-waiter looked at me askance as I sat down.

He made several trips into the kitchen before he finally came up to me and said, "The cook wants to see you." I said, "Please send the cook out here, then." He did. The cook was a Negro. The cook said, "That Filipino wants me to tell you that you can't eat in here, but I am not going to tell you no such thing. I am going to send your lunch out." He did. I ate.

Another time during the war, before they had those curtained-off tables for colored folk in Southern diners, passing through Alabama, I went to dinner and sat down in the very center of the car. The white steward leaned over and whispered politely in my ear, "Are you Negro or foreign, sir?" I said, "I'm just hungry!" The colored waiters laughed. He went away. And I was served. Sometimes a little nerve will put discrimination to rout. A dignified lady of color one day walked into a white apartment house elevator whose policy was not to take Negroes upstairs except on the servant's lift. The elevator man directed her, "Take the service car, please." She drew herself up to her full height and said, "How dare you?" He did not dare further. He took her up without a word to the white friends on whom she was calling.

A little daring with languages, too, will often go a long way. *"Dame un boletto Pullman to Chicago,"* will get you a berth in Texas when often plain English, "Give me a Pullman ticket to Chicago," will not. Negroes do not always have to change color to fool our white folks. Just change tongues. Upon returning from Europe one summer, a mulatto lady I know decided to live downtown for the winter. So, using her French, she registered at a Fifth Avenue hotel that has never before nor since been known to house a Negro guest. But she stayed there several months before moving back to Harlem. A little, *"S'il vous plait"* did it. I once knew a West Indian Negro darker than I am who spent two weeks at the Beverly-Wiltshire Hotel in the movie colony simply by registering as a Chinese from Hong Kong.

Our white folks are very easily fooled. Being so simple about race, why shouldn't they be? They have no business being prejudiced with so much democracy around. But since they are prejudiced, there's no harm in fooling the devil, is there? That old mistress in slavery time with plenty of dough, had no business denying her house servants a few biscuits. That they got them in the end served her right. Most colored folks think that as long as white folks remain foolish, prejudiced and racially selfish, they deserve to be fooled. No better for them!

George S. Schuyler (1895-   )

What the Negro
Thinks of the South

No anthology of essays by black Americans is complete without a sample of the work of one of the many columnists who have published in the Negro newspapers. One of the better-known columnists is George Schuyler, who was born in Providence, Rhode Island, and educated in the public schools of Syracuse, New York. A member of the editorial staff of *The Messenger*, from 1923 to 1928, and assistant editor from 1926 to 1928, Schuyler became more widely known as associate editor and regular columnist for *The Pittsburgh Courier*, whose editorial staff he joined in 1924. He also wrote *Slaves, Today: A History of Liberia* (1931) and *Black No More*, a satirical novel about the confusions resulting from the discovery of a drug which enables Negroes to become white.

A journalist of strong convictions, Schuyler spared neither blacks nor whites from his vitriolic ridicule. His increasing conservatism late in his career alienated many black readers who had admired his early work. In the following selection, Schuyler, a Northerner, turns his attention to Negroes' attitudes about Southern white people

What the Negro Thinks of the South

Wide circulation has been given to the opinion of the white South about the Negro but the latter's opinion of the white South has enjoyed far less currency, except in the Negro press.

Accordingly, many of our native Caucasians who have recently begun reading Negro newspapers have been quite shocked by the bitterness with which Dixie is customarily discussed, and professional Southerners of the Rankin stripe have hastened to reassert with emotional conviction the Negrophobic faiths which motivate them.

Just what do Negroes, by and large, think about the South?

Well, their thoughts about Dixie are similar to the opinion of Jews about Germany. They love the South (especially if they are Southern-born) for its beauty, its climate, its fecundity and its better ways of life; but they hate, with a bitter, corroding hatred, the color prejudice, the discrimination, the violence, the crudities, the insults and humiliations, and the racial segregation of the South, and they hate all those who keep these evils alive.

As a young Florida bootblack once told me, "The South sure would be a fine place if there wasn't no white folks there!"

I know a colored woman, a Georgia-born graduate of Spelman College who has resided in New York City for ten years. When she recently returned from a brief visit to her native State, I asked her what she thought of the South. Grimly she replied, "I would like to see it blasted by robot bombs until not a building was left standing!"

This is a rather extreme expression of the hatred of Dixie which I believe to be characteristic of most Southern Negroes living outside the South. Because of this feeling they have left there in droves and have no intention of returning except for brief visits to their families.

When these Negroes left the South they were through with it forever. They hate it for what they suffered physically and spiritually, and they are eager contributors to all efforts to fight the things for which the South stands in their opinion. In the main their paramount desire is to get their families and friends out of the South to freer territory where they will no longer be "boys," "gals" and "niggers"; where they will be free of the atmosphere of restriction, proscription and terror; where they can escape the maddeningly smug assumption of white superiority, and the oily and transparent condescension of "good" white folks who have "always loved the Negro."

Most Southern whites would be surprised to know that the Negroes who live in the South are similarly detestful of the "institutions" of Dixie. They bitterly resent having to swallow their pride, having perforce to plead and fawn for a measure of justice and fair play, having to be ever watchful of word and action for fear of swift reprisal, having forever to play second fiddle and pretend to like it.

And they loathe those Negroes in the vulnerable position of leadership who, for various reasons, pretend to like it and are sometimes wont to console themselves with the baseless belief that those who have escaped to freer soil are actually worse off, voluminous statistics to the contrary notwithstanding.

Most of these Southern Negroes feel themselves in a battle as important as any struggles of the various European Undergrounds — a battle which thy have fought in various ways for three centuries, first by poison, fire, bullet and flight, and latterly by education and organization.

For this reason they have flocked to the National Association for the Advancement of Colored People, some of whose largest and most militant branches today are below "The Line." They have rallied enthusiastically to the fight for equalization of teachers' salaries, for a free ballot, for economic advantages, and against insult, humiliation and terrorism.

The Southern Negro today regards most of the white South as his enemy, and all his scheming, planning, organizing and fighting is with the aim of worsting this enemy about whom he is far more bitter than he is against either the Germans or the Japanese.

He does not think of the white Southerners as in any way superior, save in military, political and economic power, and he has no desire to take advantage of them, assuming he could. In fact my observation has been that the Southern Negro wants as little as possible to do with the Southern white man — he simply wants the same rights, privileges and duties, and hates those who deny them to him.

As for Northern-born Negroes, they think of the South as an outlandish and barbaric area to be shunned as one would the plague, and to never visit except as a school teacher or on business. A Negro who migrates South is as rare as a Jew seeking transportation to Berlin.

They hate the white South from afar and contribute to all attacks against it with grim and fanatical zeal. For decades they fostered and sustained the attack against the enemy until their Southern brethren were prepared to join in the attack, as they have done in increasing numbers since World War I.

The average Negro does not think that *all* Southern whites are ignorant, prejudiced, cruel and unfair. He knows there are notable exceptions, but he also thinks they are a microscopic minority having little or no effect on Southern traditions and institutions.

He would like to see the South change but he is none too optimistic. He is hopeful but not gullible.

He is bitterly militant and determined, sore and resentful, and what he privately thinks of the South is usually unprintable.

Saunders Redding (1906-   )

American Negro Literature

In the period since World War II, Saunders Redding has been one of the more distinguished scholar-critics among Negro writers. Born in Delaware in 1906, he earned a Bachelor of Philosophy degree from Brown University. A member of Phi Beta Kappa Honor Society and a former college professor, he is currently Director of the Division of Research and Publication of the National Foundation on the Arts and the Humanities. Recipient of Guggenheim and Rockefeller Awards and the Mayflower Award from the North Carolina Literary and Historical Society for his autobiographical *No Day of Triumph*, Redding has published a novel, *Stranger and Alone* (1950); an excellent critical history of literature by Negroes, *To Make a Poet Black* (1939); a collection of essays, *On Being Negro in America* (1951); and three histories of Negroes in America. His most recent book is *The Negro* (1967).

As a frequent contributor to periodicals, Redding has earned a reputation as a perceptive and knowledgeable historian of literature by Afro-Americans. The following selection summarizes their literary development during the first half of the twentieth century.

American Negro Literature

There is this about literature by American Negroes — it has uncommon resilience. Three times within this century it has been

Reprinted from *The American Scholar,* Volume 18, Number 2, Spring, 1949. Copyright ©1949 by the United Chapters of Phi Beta Kappa. By permission of the publishers.

done nearly to death: once by indifference, once by opposition, and once by the unbounded enthusiasm of its well-meaning friends.

By 1906, Charles W. Chesnutt, the best writer of prose fiction the race had produced, was silent; Paul Laurence Dunbar, the most popular poet, was dead. After these two, at least in the general opinion, there were no other Negro writers. Booker Washington had published *Up from Slavery*, but Washington was no writer — he was the orator and the organizer of the march to a questionable new Canaan. The poetic prose of DuBois, throbbing in *The Souls of Black Folk*, had not yet found its audience. Polemicists like Monroe Trotter, Kelly Miller, and George Forbes were faint whispers in a lonesome wood. Indifference had stopped the ears of all but the most enlightened who, as often as not, were derisively labeled "nigger lovers."

But this indifference had threatened even before the turn of the century. Dunbar felt it, and the purest stream of his lyricism was made bitter and all but choked by it. Yearning for the recognition of his talent as it expressed itself in the pure English medium, he had to content himself with a kindly, but condescending praise of his dialect pieces. Time and again he voiced the sense of frustration brought on by the neglect of what he undoubtedly considered his best work. Writing dialect, he told James Weldon Johnson, was "the only way he could get them to listen to him." His literary friend and sponsor, William D. Howells, at that time probably the most influential critic in America, passing over Dunbar's verse in pure English with only a glance, urged him to write "of his own race in its own accents of our English."

During Dunbar's lifetime, his pieces in pure English appeared more or less on sufferance. The very format of the 1901 edition of *Lyrics of the Hearthside*, the book in which most of his non-dialect poetry was published, suggests this. No fancy binding on this book, no handsome paper, no charming, illustrative photographs. *Lyrics of the Hearthside* was the least publicized of all his books of poetry, and four lines from his "The Poet" may tell why.

> He sang of love when earth was young,
> And love itself was in his lays,
> But, ah, the world it turned to praise
> A jingle in a broken tongue.

Enough has been said about the false concepts, the stereotypes which were effective — and to some extent are still effective — in white America's thinking about the Negro for the point not to be labored here. History first, and then years of insidious labor to perpetuate what history had wrought, created these stereotypes. According to them, the Negro was a buffoon, a harmless child of nature, a dangerous despoiler (the concepts were contradictory), an irresponsible beast of devilish cunning — soulless, ambitionless and depraved. The Negro, in short, was a higher species of some creature that was not quite man.

What this had done to writing by American Negroes could easily be imagined, even without the documentation, which is abundant. No important critic of writing by American Negroes has failed to note the influence of the concept upon it. Sterling Brown, one of the more searching scholars in the field, gives it scathing comment in "The Negro Author and His Publisher." James Weldon Johnson touches upon it in his preface to the 1931 edition of his anthology, but he does so even more cogently in "The Negro Author's Dilemma." The introduction to Countee Cullen's *Caroling Dusk* is a wry lament over it. In *The New Negro*, Alain Locke expresses the well-founded opinion that the Negro "has been a stock figure perpetuated as an historical fiction partly in innocent sentimentalism, partly in deliberate reactionism."

There can be no question as to the power of the traditional concepts. The Negro writer reacted to them in one of two ways. Either he bowed down to them, writing such stories as would do them no violence; or he went to the opposite extreme and wrote for the purpose of invalidating, or at least denying, the tradition. Dunbar did the former. Excepting only a few, his short stories depict Negro characters as whimsical, simple, folksy, not-too-bright souls, all of whose social problems are little ones, and all of whose emotional cares can be solved by the intellectual or spiritual equivalent of a stick of red peppermint candy. It is of course significant that three of his four novels are not about Negroes at all; and the irony of depicting himself as a white youth in his spiritual autobiography, *The Uncalled*, needs no comment.

Charles Chesnutt's experience is also to the point. When his stories began appearing in the *Atlantic Monthly* in 1887, it was not generally known that their author was a Negro. Stories like "The Gray Wolf's Ha'nt" and "The Goophered Grapevine" were so detached and objective that the author's race could not have been detected from a reading of them. The editor of the *Atlantic Monthly*, Walter H. Page, fearing that public acknowledgment of it would do the author's work harm, was reluctant to admit that Chesnutt was a Negro, and the fact of his race was kept a closely guarded secret for a decade.

It was this same fear that led to the rejection of Chesnutt's first novel, *The House Behind The Cedars,* for "a literary work by an American of acknowledged color was a doubtful experiment . . . entirely apart from its intrinsic merit." The reception of Chesnutt's later books — those that came after 1900 — was to prove that literary works by an "American of color" were more than doubtful experiments. *The Colonel's Dream* and *The Marrow of Tradition* did not pay the cost of the paper and the printing. They were honest probings at the heart of a devilish problem; they were, quite frankly, propaganda. But the thing that made the audience of the day indifferent to them was their attempt to override the concepts that were the props of the dialect tradition. Had Chesnutt not had a reputation as a writer of short stories (which are, anyway, his best work), it is likely that his novels would not have been published at all.

The poetry of Dunbar and the prose of Chesnutt proved that even with the arbitrary limitations imposed upon them by historical convention, Negro writers could rise to heights of artistic expression. They could even circumvent the convention, albeit self-consciously, and create credible white characters in a credible white milieu.

II

After about 1902, indifference began to crystallize into opposition to the culture-conscious, race-conscious Negro seeking honest answers to honest questions. It was opposition to the Negro's democratic ambitions which were just then beginning to burgeon. It was opposition to the Negro who was weary of his role of clown, scapegoat, doormat. And it was, of course, opposition to the Negro writer who was honest and sincere and anxious beyond the bounds of superimposed racial polity.

There is danger here of over-simplifying a long and complex story. Even with the advantage of hindsight, it is hard to tell what is cause and what effect. But let us have a look at some of the more revealing circumstances. In 1902 came Thomas Dixon's *The Leopard's Spots,* and three years later *The Clansman.* They were both tremendously popular. In 1906 there were race riots in Georgia and Texas, in 1908 in Illinois. . . . By this later year, too, practically all of the Southern states had disfranchised the Negro and made color caste legal. . . . The Negro's talent for monkeyshines had been exploited on the stage, and coon songs (some by James Weldon Johnson and his brother!) had attained wide popularity. Meantime, in 1904, Thomas Nelson Page had published the bible of reactionism, *The Negro, The Southerner's Problem.* And, probably most cogent fact of all, Booker Washington had reached the position of undisputed leader of American Negroes by advocating a racial policy strictly in line with the traditional concept.

There had been a time when the old concept of the Negro had served to ease his burden. He had been laughed at, tolerated, and genially despaired of as hopeless in a modern, dynamic society. White Americans had become used to a myth — had, indeed, convinced themselves that myth was reality. All the instruments of social betterment — schools, churches, lodges — adopted by colored people were the subjects of ribald jokes and derisive laughter. Even the fact that the speeches which Booker Washington was making up and down the country could have been made only by a really intelligent and educated man did not strike them as a contradiction of the concept. And anyway, there was this about Washington: he was at least half-white, and white blood in that proportion excused and accounted for many a thing, including being intelligent, lunching with President Theodore Roosevelt, and getting an honorary degree from Harvard.

Today any objective judgment of Booker Washington's basic notion must be that it was an extension of the old tradition framed in new terms. He preached a message of compromise, of humility, of patience. Under the impact of social change the concept was modified to include the stereotype of the Negro as satisfied peasant, a docile servitor under the stern but kindly eye of the white boss; a creature who had a place, knew it, and would keep it unless he got *bad* notions from somewhere. The merely laughable coon had become also the cheap laborer who could be righteously exploited for his own good and to the greater glory of God. By this addition to the concept, the Negro-white status quo — the condition of inferior-superior caste — could be maintained in the face of profound changes in the general society.

What this meant to the Negro artist and writer was that he must, if he wished an audience, adhere to the old forms and the acceptable patterns. It meant that he must work within the limitations of the concept, or ignore his racial kinship altogether and leave unsounded the profoundest depths of the peculiar experiences which were his by reason of his race. But fewer and fewer Negro writers were content with the limitations. The num-

ber of dialect pieces (the term includes the whole tradition)
written after 1907 is very small indeed. Among Negro writers the
tradition had lost its force and its validity. White writers like
Julia Peterkin and Gilmore Millen, and, in a different way, Carl
Van Vechten and DuBose Heyward, were to lend it a spurious
strength down through the 1920's.

Negro writers of unmistakable talent chose the second course,
and some of them won high critical praise for their work in
non-racial themes. Their leader was William Stanley Braithwaite.
Save only a few essays written at the behest of his friend,
W. E. B. DuBois, nothing that came from his pen had anything
about it to mark it as Negro. His leading essays in the Boston
Transcript, his anthologies of magazine verse, and his own poetry,
might just as well have been written by someone with no background in the provocative experience of being colored in America.

Though the other Negro poets of this genre (which was not
entirely a genre) developed a kind of dilettantist virtuosity, none
carried it to Braithwaite's amazing lengths of self-conscious con-
trivance. They were simpler and more conventional in their apostasy. Alice Dunbar, the widow of Paul, wrote sonnets of uncommon
skill and beauty. Georgia Johnson and Anne Spenser were at
home in the formal lyric, and James Weldon Johnson in "The
White Witch" and "My City" set a very high standard for his
fellow contributors to the *Century Magazine*.

But given the whole web of circumstance — empirical, historic,
racial, psychological — these poets must have realized that they
could not go on in this fashion. With a full tide of race-con-
sciousness bearing in upon them individually and as a group, they
could not go on forever denying their racehood. To try to do
this at all was symptomatic of neurotic strain. They could not
go on, and they did not. The hardiest of them turned to expression
of another kind the moment the pressure was off.

The pressure was not off for another decade and a half. As a
matter of fact, it mounted steadily. For all of Booker Washington's popularity and ideological appeal among whites, who had
set him up as *the* leader of the Negro race, and for all of his
power, there was rebellion against him in the forward ranks of
Negroes. Rebellion against Washington meant dissatisfaction with
the social and economic goals which he had persuaded white
Americans were the proper goals for the Negro race. The whites
had not counted on this disaffection, and their reaction to it was
willful, blind opposition.

What had happened was that Booker Washington, with the
help of the historic situation and the old concept, had so thor-

oughly captured the minds of most of those white people who were kindly disposed to Negroes that not another Negro had a chance to be heard. Negro schools needing help could get it from rich and powerful whites only through Booker Washington. Negro social thought wanting a sounding board could have it only with the sanction of the principal of Tuskegee. Negro politicians were helpless without his endorsement. Negro seekers after jobs of any consequence in either public or private capacities begged recommendations from Booker Washington.

This despotic power — and there is scarcely another term for it — was stultifying to many intelligent Negroes, especially in the North. White editors, who would have published anything under the signature of Booker Washington, consistently rejected all but the most innocuous work of other Negroes. Publishers were not interested in the ideas of Negroes unless those ideas conformed to Washington's, or in creative work by and about Negroes unless they fell into the old pattern.

So intelligent, articulate Negroes grew insurgent, and the leader of this insurgence was W. E. B. DuBois. Nor was his the only voice raised in protest. Charles Chesnutt spoke out, and so did John Hope and Kelly Miller. In 1900 the *Chicago Defender* had been founded, and in 1901 Monroe Trotter's *Boston Guardian*. Courageous as these polemical organs were, they had not yet grown into full effectiveness. Neither had DuBois, but he was growing fast. By 1903 the Atlanta University Studies of the Negro were coming out regularly under his editorship. In that year he published *The Souls of Black Folk*, which contained the essay "Of Mr. Booker T. Washington and Others," sharply critical of the Tuskegee leader. DuBois was in on the founding of the National Association for the Advancement of Colored People, and in 1910 he became editor of the new monthly, the *Crisis*.

From the very first the *Crisis* was much more than the official organ of the N.A.A.C.P. It was a platform for the expression of all sorts of ideas that ran counter to the notion of Negro inferiority. Excepting such liberal and nonpopular journals as the *Atlantic Monthly* and *World's Work* and the two or three Negro newspapers that had not been bought or throttled by the "Tuskegee Machine," the *Crisis* was the only voice the Negro had. The opposition to that voice was organized around the person and the philosophy of Booker Washington, and there were times when this opposition all but drowned out the voice.

Nevertheless protestation and revolt were becoming bit by bit more powerful reagents in the social chemistry that produced the New Negro. Year by year more Negroes were transformed — and a lot of them needed transforming. Once James Weldon Johnson himself had written "coon songs" and been content to carol with sweet humility "Lift Every Voice and Sing." When Johnson wrote it in 1900, it had the approval of Booker Washington and became the "Negro National Anthem." Then followed Johnson's period of apostasy and such jejune pieces as "The Glory of the Day Was in Her Face," among others. But in 1912, when he was already forty-one, he wrote the novel *The Autobiography of an Ex-Colored Man,* and in 1917 he cried out bitterly that Negroes must cease speaking "servile words" and must "stand erect and without fear."

III

Other factors than simple protest contributed to the generation of the New Negro. In the first place, the notions regarding the Old Negro were based on pure myth. The changes occurring at the onset of war in Europe sloughed off some of the emotional and intellectual accretions, and the Negro stood partially revealed for what he was — a fellow whose opportunities had been narrowed by historical fallacies, "a creature of moral debate," but a man pretty much as other men. The war, which made him an inter-sectional migrant, proved that he, too, sought more economic opportunities, the protection of laws even-handedly administered, the enlargement of democracy. He, too, was a seeker for the realities in the American dream.

But when in 1917 the Negro was called upon to protect that dream with his blood, he revealed himself more fully. He asked questions and demanded answers. Whose democracy? he wanted to know; and why, and wherefore? There followed the promises, which were certainly sincerely meant in the stress of the times. Then came the fighting and dying — and, finally, came a thing called Peace. But in 1919 and after, there were the race riots in the nation's capital, in Chicago, in Chester, Pennsylvania, and in East St. Louis.

By this time the New Negro movement was already stirring massively along many fronts. In the 1920's Negroes cracked through the prejudices that had largely confined them to supernumerary roles on Broadway. *Shuffle Along* was praised as "a sparkling, all-Negro musical of unusual zest and talent." Charles Gilpin's portrayal of the Emperor Jones was the dramatic triumph of 1921. The Garvey Movement, fast getting out of bounds, swept the country like a wildfire. James Weldon Johnson published an anthology of Negro verse. The monumental historical studies of the Negro were begun by Carter Woodson. *The Gift of Black Folk, Color, Fire in the Flint, Weary Blues, God's Trombones, Walls of Jericho,* and *Home to Harlem* had all been published, read, discussed, praised or damned by 1928.

Fortunately some of the talents that produced these works were genuine. Had this not been so, the New Negro movement in art and literature would surely have come to nothing. The best of Johnson, Hughes, Cullen, McKay, Fisher and DuBois would have lived without the movement, but the movement without them would have gone the way of mah-jongg. Their work considerably furthered the interest of white writers and critics in Negro material and Negro art expression. Whatever else Eugene O'Neill, Paul Rosenfeld and DuBose Heyward did, they gave validity to the new concept of the Negro as material for serious artistic treatment.

Writing by Negroes beginning with this period and continuing into the early thirties had two distinct aspects. The first of these was extremely arty, self-conscious and experimental. Jean Toomer's *Cane* and the "racial-rhythm" and jazz-rhythm poetry of Langston Hughes represent it most notably, while the magazines *Harlem* and *Fire,* which published a quantity of nonsense by writers unheard of since, were its special organs. But the times were themselves arty and experimental. That Negro writers could afford to be touched by these influences was a good sign. It was healthy for them to be blown upon by the winds of literary freedom—even of license — that blew upon e. e. cummings, Dos Passos and Hemingway. If their self-conscious experimentation proved nothing lasting, it at least worked no harm.

One searches in vain for a phrase to characterize the exact impulses behind the second aspect, which is the one best remembered. It was chock-full of many contradictory things. It showed itself naive and sophisticated, hysterical and placid, frivolous and sober, free and enslaved. It is simple enough to attribute this contrariety to the effects of the war; but the atavistic release of certain aberrant tendencies in writing by Negroes in this period cannot be matched in all the rest of contemporary writing. The period produced the poignant beauty of Johnson's *God's Trombones* and the depressing futility of Thurman's *The Blacker The Berry.* Within a span of five years McKay wrote the wholesome

Banjo and the pointlessly filthy *Banana Bottom*. The Hughes who wrote "I've Known Rivers" and "Mother to Son" could also find creative satisfaction in the bizarre "The Cat and the Saxophone."

The mass mind of white America fastened upon the exotic and the atavistic elements and fashioned them into a fad, the commercialized products of which were manufactured in Harlem. That that Harlem itself was largely synthetic did not seem to matter. It was "nigger heaven." There, the advertised belief was, Dullness was dethroned: Gaiety was king! The rebels from Sauk Center and Winesburg, Main Street and Park Avenue, sought carnival in Harlem. "Life," the burden of the dithyrambics ran, "had surge and sweep there, and blood-pounding savagery."

Commercialism was the bane of the Negro renaissance of the twenties. Jazz music became no longer the uninhibited expression of unlearned music-makers, but a highly sophisticated pattern of musical sounds. The "Charleston" and the "Black Bottom" went down to Broadway and Park Avenue. Losing much of its folk value, the blues became the "torch song" eloquently sung by Ruth Etting and Helen Morgan. Negro material passed into the less sincere hands of white artists, and Negro writers themselves, from a high pitch of creation, fell relatively and pathetically silent.

IV

When Richard Wright's *Uncle Tom's Children* was published in 1938, only the least aware did not realize that a powerful new pen was employing itself in stern and terrible material; when *Native Son* appeared in 1940, even the least aware realized it. The first book is a clinical study of human minds under the stress of violence; the second is a clinical study of the social being under the cumulative effects of organized repression. The two books complement each other. The theme of both is prejudice, conceptual prejudgment — the effects of this upon the human personality. For Wright deals only incidentally — and for dramatic purposes, and because of the authenticity of empiricism — with *Negro* and *white*. "Bigger Thomas was not black all the time," Wright wrote in "How Bigger Was Born." "He was white, too, and there were literally millions of him, *everywhere*. . . . Certain modern experiences were creating types of personalities whose existence ignored racial and national lines. . . ."

Some critics have said that the wide appeal of Wright's work (it has been translated into a dozen languages) is due to the sensationalism in it, but one can have serious doubts that the sensationalism comes off well in translation. What does come off well is the concept of the primary evil of prejudice. This all peoples would understand, and a delineation of its effects, particular though it be, interests them in the same way and for the same reason that love interests them. *Black Boy*, which does not prove the point, does not deny it either. Even here it may be argued that Wright delineates and skewers home the point that "to live habitually as a superior among inferiors . . . is a temptation and a hubris, inevitably deteriorating."

So Wright is a new kind of writer in the ranks of Negroes. He has extricated himself from the dilemma of writing exclusively for a Negro audience and limiting himself to a glorified and race-proud picture of Negro life, and of writing exclusively for a white audience and being trapped in the old stereotypes and fixed opinions that are bulwarks against honest creation. Negro writers traditionally have been impaled upon one or the other horn of this dilemma, sometimes in spite of their efforts to avoid it. Langston Hughes was sincere when he declared, back in the twenties, that Negro writers cared nothing for the pleasure or displeasure of either a white or a colored audience — he was sincere, but mistaken.

A writer writes for an audience. Until recently Negro writers have not believed that the white audience and the colored audience were essentially alike, because, in fact, they have not been essentially alike. They have been kept apart by a wide socio-cultural gulf, by differences of concept, by cultivated fears, ignorance, race- and caste-consciousness. Now that gulf is closing, and Negro writers are finding it easier to appeal to the two audiences without being either false to the one or subservient to the other. Thus Margaret Walker, writing for the two audiences now becoming one, can carry away an important poetry prize with her book *For My People*. No longer fearing the ancient interdiction, Chester Himes in *If He Hollers Let Him Go* and *Lonely Crusade* writes of the sexual attraction a white woman feels for a Negro man. In *Knock On Any Door* Willard Motley can concern himself almost entirely with white characters. On the purely romantic and escapist side, Frank Yerby's *The Foxes of Harrow* sells over a million copies, and *The Vixens* and *The Golden Hawk* over a half-million each. Anthologists no longer think it risky to collect, edit and issue the works of Negro writers.

Facing up to the tremendous challenge of appealing to two audiences, Negro writers are extricating themselves from what has sometimes seemed a terrifying dilemma. Working honestly in the material they know best, they are creating for themselves a new freedom. Though what is happening seems very like a miracle, it has been a long, long time preparing. Writing by American Negroes has never before been in such a splendid state of health, nor had so bright and shining a future before it.

Ralph Ellison (1914-   )

On Becoming A Writer

Ralph Ellison is widely known in the academic world as the author of *Invisible Man* (1952), a work which some critics consider the most artistic novel written by a Negro American. In 1964 a group of 200 American writers and editors voted it the most distinguished novel written by any American in the past twenty years.

Born in Oklahoma, Ellison studied music at Tuskegee Institute; but, after going to New York in the summer following his junior year, he never returned to college. In New York, he worked at various jobs, for a time performed as a professional jazz musician, and began writing articles and reviews for various magazines. Despite his continuous productivity as a writer, he did not earn critical attention until he published *Invisible Man*, on which he had labored for seven years. Since then, he has taught at various colleges, worked on a second novel, and continued to produce essays. In 1964 he published *Shadow and Act*, a collection of essays and interviews.

Ironically, although Ellison's literary reputation derives from his novel, the bulk of his writing is essay — reviews, critical appraisals of writers and musicians, analyses and discussions of jazz, and reminiscences. In these, especially in "Richard Wright's Blues," he has revealed his keen insights into aesthetics, jazz,

Originally published in *Commentary* (October 1964). ©Copyright 1964 by Ralph Ellison. Another version appears in *Shadow and Act* by Ralph Ellison. Reprinted by permission of Random House.

blues, and literature, always phrased in a style suggestive of the academic scholar rather than the professional writer. In his most recent writing, Ellison frequently has stressed two themes: the necessity that America recognize and respect the cultural identity of black Americans and the need for Negroes to understand the labor that is required for success.

In the following selection, he recalls his search for and discovery of identity as a writer.

On Becoming A Writer

In the beginning writing was far from a serious matter; it was a reflex of reading, an extension of a source of pleasure, escape, and instruction. In fact, I had become curious about writing by way of seeking to understand the aesthetic nature of literary power, the devices through which literature could command my mind and emotions. It was not, then, the *process* of writing which initially claimed my attention, but the finished creations, the artifacts, poems, plays, novels. The act of learning writing technique was, therefore, an amusing investigation of what seemed at best a secondary talent, an exploration, like dabbling in sculpture, of one's potentialities as a "Renaissance Man." This, surely, would seem a most unlikely and even comic concept to introduce here; and yet, it is precisely because I come from where I do (the Oklahoma of the years between World War I and the Great Depression) that I must introduce it, and with a straight face.

Anything and everything was to be found in the chaos of Oklahoma; thus the concept of the Renaissance Man has lurked long within the shadow of my past, and I shared it with at least a half dozen of my Negro friends. How we actually acquired it I have never learned, and since there is no true sociology of the dispersion of ideas within the American democracy, I doubt if I ever shall. Perhaps we breathed it in with the air of the Negro community of Oklahoma City, the capital of that state whose Negroes were often charged by exasperated white Texans with not knowing their "place." Perhaps we took it defiantly from one of them. Or perhaps I myself picked it up from some transplanted New Englander whose shoes I had shined of a Saturday afternoon. After all, the most meaningful tips do not always come in the form of money, nor are they intentionally extended. Most likely, however, my friends and I acquired the idea from some book or from some idealistic Negro teacher, some dreamer seeking to function responsibly in an environment which at its most normal took on some of the mixed character of nightmare and of dream.

One thing is certain, ours was a chaotic community, still characterized by frontier attitudes and by that strange mixture of the naive and sophisticated, the benign and malignant, which makes the American past so puzzling and its present so confusing; that mixture which often affords the minds of the young who grow up in the far provinces such wide and unstructured latitude, and which encourages the individual's imagination — up to the moment "reality" closes in upon him — to range widely and, sometimes, even to soar.

We hear the effects of this in the Southwestern jazz of the 30's, that joint creation of artistically free and exhuberantly creative adventurers, of artists who had stumbled upon the freedom lying within the restrictions of their musical tradition as within the limitations of their social background, and who in their own unconscious way have set an example for any Americans, Negro or white, who would find themselves in the arts. They accepted themselves and the complexity of life as they knew it, they loved their art and through it they celebrated American experience definitively in sound. Whatever others thought or felt, this was their own powerful statement, and only non-musical assaults upon their artistic integrity — mainly economically inspired changes of fashion — were able to compromise their vision.

Much of so-called Kansas City jazz was actually brought to perfection in Oklahoma by Oklahomans. It is an important circumstance for me as a writer to remember, because while these musicians and their fellows were busy creating out of tradition, imagination, and the sounds and emotions around them, a freer, more complex, and driving form of jazz, my friends and I were exploring an idea of human versatility and possibility which went against the barbs or over the palings of almost every fence which those who controlled social and political power had erected to restrict our roles in the life of the country. Looking back, one might say that the jazzmen, some of whom we idolized, were in their own way better examples for youth to follow than were most judges and ministers, legislators and governors (we were stuck with the notorious Alfalfa Bill Murray). For as we viewed these pillars of society from the confines of our segregated community we almost always saw crooks, clowns, or hypocrites. Even the best were revealed by their attitudes toward us as lacking the respectable qualities to which they pretended and for which they were accepted outside by others, while despite the outlaw nature of their art, the jazzmen were less torn and damaged by the moral compromises and insincerities which have so sickened the life of our country.

Be that as it may, our youthful sense of life, like that of many Negro children (though no one bothers to note it — especially the specialists and "friends of the Negro" who view our Negro-American life as essentially non-human) was very much like that of Huckleberry Finn, who is universally so praised and enjoyed for the clarity and courage of his moral vision. Like Huck, we observed, we judged, we imitated and evaded as we could the dullness, corruption, and blindness of "civilization." We were undoubtedly comic because, as the saying goes, we weren't supposed to know what it was all about. But to ourselves we were "boys," members of a wild, free, outlaw tribe which transcended the category of race. Rather we were Americans born into the forty-sixth state, and thus, into the context of Negro-American post-Civil War history, "frontiersmen." And isn't one of the implicit functions of the American frontier to encourage the individual to a kind of dreamy wakefulness, a state in which he makes — in all ignorance of the accepted limitations of the possible — rash efforts, quixotic gestures, hopeful testings of the complexity of the known and the given?

Spurring us on in our controlled and benign madness was the voracious reading of which most of us were guilty and the vicarious identification and empathetic adventuring which it encouraged. This was due, in part, perhaps to the fact that some of us were fatherless — my own father had died when I was three — but most likely it was because boys are natural romantics. We were seeking examples, patterns to live by, out of a freedom which for all its being ignored by the sociologists and subtle thinkers, was implicit in the Negro situation. Father and mother substitutes also have a role to play in aiding the child to help create himself. Thus we fabricated our own heroes and ideals catch-as-catch-can; and with an outrageous and irreverent sense of freedom. Yes, and in complete disregard of ideas of respectability or the surreal incongruity of some of our projections. Gamblers and scholars, jazz musicians and scientists, Negro cowboys and soldiers from the Spanish-American and First World Wars, movie stars and stunt men, figures from the Italian Renaissance and literature, both classical and popular, were combined with the special virtues' of some local bootlegger, the eloquence of some Negro preacher, the strength and grace of some local athlete, the ruthlessness of some businessman-physician, the elegance in dress and manners of some head-waiter or hotel doorman.

Looking back through the shadows upon this absurd activity, I realize now that we were projecting archetypes, recreating folk figures, legendary heroes, monsters even, most of which violated all ideas of social hierarchy and order and all accepted conceptions of the hero handed down by cultural, religious, and racist tradition. But we, remember, were under the intense spell of the early movies, the silents as well as the talkies; and in our community, life was not so tightly structured as it would have been in the traditional South — or even in deceptively "free" Harlem. And our imaginations processed reality and dream, natural man and traditional hero, literature and folklore, like maniacal editors turned loose in some frantic film-cutting room. Remember, too, that being boys, yet in the play-stage of our development, we were dream-serious in our efforts. But serious nevertheless, for *culturally* play is a preparation, and we felt that somehow the human ideal lay in the vague and constantly shifting figures — sometimes comic but always versatile, picaresque, and self-effacingly heroic — which evolved from our wildly improvisatory projections: figures neither white nor black, Christian nor Jewish, but representative of certain desirable essences, of skills and powers, physical, aesthetic, and moral.

The proper response to these figures was, we felt, to develop ourselves for the performance of many and diverse roles, and the fact that certain definite limitations had been imposed upon our freedom did not lessen our sense of obligation. Not only were we to prepare but we were to perform — not with mere competence but with an almost reckless verve; with, may we say (without evoking the quaint and questionable notion of *négritude*) Negro-American style? Behind each artist there stands a traditional sense of style, a sense of the felt tension indicative of expressive completeness; a mode of humanizing reality and of evoking a feeling of being at home in the world. It is something which the artist shares with the group, and part of our boyish activity expressed a yearning to make any and everything of quality

Negro-American; to appropriate it, possess it, recreate it in our own group and individual images.

And we recognized and were proud of our group's own style wherever we discerned it, in jazzmen and prize-fighters, ballplayers, and tap dancers; in gesture, inflection, intonation, timbre, and phrasing. Indeed, in all those nuances of expression and attitude which reveal a culture. We did not fully understand the cost of that style, but we recognized within it an affirmation of life beyond all question of our difficulties as Negroes.

Contrary to the notion currently projected by certain specialists in the "Negro problem" which characterizes the Negro American as self-hating and defensive, we did not so regard ourselves. We felt, among ourselves at least, that we were supposed to be whoever we would and could be and do anything and everything which other boys did, and do it better. Not defensively, because we were ordered to do so; nor because it was held in the society at large that we were naturally, as Negroes, limited — but because we demanded it of ourselves. Because to measure up to our own standards was the only way of affirming our notion of manhood.

Hence it was no more incongruous, as seen from our own particular perspective in this land of incongruities, for young Negro Oklahomans to project themselves as Renaissance men than for white Mississippians to see themselves as ancient Greeks or noblemen out of Sir Walter Scott. Surely our fantasies have caused far less damage to the nation's sense of reality, if for no other reason than that ours were expressive of a more democratic ideal. Remember, too, as William Faulkner made us so vividly aware, that the slaves often took the essence of the aristocratic ideal (as they took Christianity) with far more seriousness than their masters, and that we, thanks to the tight telescoping of American history, were but two generations from that previous condition. Renaissance men, indeed!

I managed, by keeping quiet about it, to cling to our boyish ideal during three years in Alabama, and I brought it with me to New York, where it not only gave silent support to my explorations of what was then an unknown territory, but served to mock and caution me when I became interested in the Communist ideal. And when it was suggested that I try my hand at writing it was still with me.

The act of writing requires a constant plunging back into the shadow of the past where time hovers ghostlike. When I began writing in earnest I was forced, thus, to relate myself consciously and imaginatively to my mixed background as American, as Negro-American, and as a Negro from what in its own belated way was a pioneer background. More important, and inseparable from this particular effort, was the necessity of determining my true relationship to that body of American literature to which I was most attracted and through which, aided by what I could learn from the literatures of Europe, I would find my own voice and to which I was challenged, by way of achieving myself, to make some small contribution, and to whose composite picture of reality I was obligated to offer some necessary modifications.

This was no matter of sudden insight but of slow and blundering discovery, of a struggle to stare down the deadly and hypnotic temptation to interpret the world and all its devices in terms of race. To avoid this was very important to me, and in light of my background far from simple. Indeed, it was quite complex, involving as it did, a ceaseless questioning of all those formulas which historians, politicians, sociologists, and an older generation of Negro leaders and writers — those of the so-called "Negro Renaissance" — had evolved to describe my group's identity, its predicament, its fate, and its relation to the larger society and the culture which we share.

Here the question of reality and personal identity merge. Yes, and the question of the nature of the reality which underlies American fiction and thus the human truth which gives fiction viability. In this quest, for such it soon became, I learned that nothing could go unchallenged; especially that feverish industry dedicated to telling Negroes who and what they are, and which can usually be counted upon to deprive both humanity and culture of their complexity. I had undergone, not too many months before taking the path which led to writing, the humiliation of being taught in a class in sociology at a Negro college (from Park and Burgess, the leading textbook in the field) that Negroes represented the "lady of the races." This contention the Negro instructor passed blandly along to us without even bothering to wash his hands, much less his teeth. Well, I had no intention of being bound by any such humiliating definition of my relationship to American literature. Not even to those works which depicted Negroes negatively. Negro Americans have a highly developed ability to abstract desirable qualities from those around them, even from their enemies, and my sense of reality could reject bias while appreciating the truth revealed by achieved art. The pleasure which I derived from reading had long been a necessity, and in the *act* of reading, that marvelous collaboration between the writer's artful vision and the reader's sense of life, I had become acquainted with other possible selves; freer, more courageous and ingenuous and, during the course of the narrative at least, even wise.

At the time I was under the influence of Ernest Hemingway, and his description, in *Death in the Afternoon,* of his thinking when he first went to Spain became very important as translated in my own naïve fashion. He was trying to write, he tells us,

> and I found the greatest difficulty aside from knowing truly what you really felt, rather than what you were supposed to feel, and had been taught to feel, was to put down what really happened in action; what the actual things were which produced the emotion that you experienced. . . .

His statement of moral and aesthetic purpose which followed focused my own search to relate myself to American life through literature. For I found the greatest difficulty for a Negro writer was the problem of revealing what he truly felt, rather than serving up what Negroes were supposed to feel, and were encouraged to feel. And linked to this was the difficulty, based upon our long habit of deception and evasion, of depicting what really happened within our areas of American life, and putting down with honesty and without bowing to ideological expediencies the attitudes and values which give Negro-American life its sense of wholeness and which render it bearable and human and, when measured by our own terms, desirable.

I was forced to this awareness through my struggles with the craft of fiction; yes, and by my attraction (soon rejected) to Marxist political theory, which was my response to the inferior status which society sought to impose upon me (I did not then, now, or ever *consider* myself inferior).

I did not know my true relationship to America — what citizen of the U.S. really does? — but I did know and accept how I felt inside. And I also knew, thanks to the old Renaissance Man, what I expected of myself in the matter of personal discipline and creative quality. Since by the grace of the past and the examples of manhood picked willy-nilly from the continuing-present of my background, I rejected all negative definitions imposed upon me by others, there was nothing to do but search for those relationships which were fundamental.

In this sense fiction became the agency of my efforts to answer the questions, Who am I, what am I, how did I come to be? What shall I make of the life around me, what celebrate, what reject, how confront the snarl of good and evil which is inevitable? What does American society *mean* when regarded out of my *own* eyes, when informed by my *own* sense of the past and viewed by my *own* complex sense of the present? How, in other words, should I think of myself and my pluralistic sense of the world, how express my vision of the human predicament, without reducing it to a point which would render it sterile before that necessary and tragic — though enhancing — reduction which must occur before the fictive vision can come alive? It is quite possible that much potential fiction by Negro Americans fails precisely at this point: through the writers' refusal (often through provincialism or lack of courage or through opportunism) to achieve a vision of life and a resourcefulness of craft commensurate with the complexity of their actual situation. Too often they fear to leave the uneasy sanctuary of race to take their chances in the world of art.

James Baldwin (1924-   )

The Discovery of What
It Means to be an American

James Baldwin is the best-known Negro writer today and one of the most distinguished essayists writing in the English language. Born in New York City and educated in the schools of that city, Baldwin, at the age of fourteen, became a minister after a religious awakening which he described in his first novel, *Go Tell It on the Mountain* (1953). After three years as a minister, Baldwin experienced disillusionment which caused him to reject Christianity. Leaving home, working at odd jobs while learning to be a writer, Baldwin finally migrated to France to search for his identity and for a new faith.

His first novel earned praise from critics who believed that they had discovered a Negro capable of writing artistically about life without revealing bitterness about the black experience. His two collections of essays, *Notes of a Native Son* (1955) and *Nobody Knows My Name* (1961) informed critics of their error but firmly established his reputation as a major essayist. In essays, Baldwin has articulated the Negro experience more effectively than any black writer since W. E. B. DuBois. Simultaneously, he has compelled many white readers to re-examine their beliefs and their attitudes.

In the early sixties, Baldwin completed three highly controversial, financially successful works on racial themes — *Another Coun-*

try (1962), a novel; *The Fire Next Time* (1963), a long essay; and *Blues for Mr. Charlie* (1964), a drama. His most recent works of fiction — *Going to Meet the Man* (1965) and *Tell Me How Long the Train's Been Gone* (1968) — have been received more ambivalently by critics, who, willing to acknowledge his stylistic excellence as an essayist, argue that he has not fulfilled his artistic promise as a writer of fiction.

The following selection is taken from Baldwin's second collection of essays. In it, Baldwin recalls how experiences in Europe helped him to understand that he was not merely Negro but also American.

The Discovery of What It Means to be an American

"It is a complex fate to be an American," Henry James observed, and the principal discovery an American writer makes in Europe is just how complex this fate is. America's history, her aspirations, her peculiar triumphs, her even more peculiar defeats, and her position in the world — yesterday and today — are all so profoundly and stubbornly unique that the very word "America" remains a new, almost completely undefined and extremely controversial proper noun. No one in the world seems to know exactly what it describes, not even we motley millions who call ourselves Americans.

I left America because I doubted my ability to survive the fury of the color problem here. (Sometimes I still do.) I wanted to prevent myself from becoming *merely* a Negro; or, even, merely a Negro writer. I wanted to find out in what way the *specialness* of my experience could be made to connect me with other people instead of dividing me from them. (I was as isolated from Negroes as I was from whites, which is what happens when a Negro begins, at bottom, to believe what white people say about him.)

In my necessity to find the terms on which my experience could be related to that of others, Negroes and whites, writers and non-writers, I proved, to my astonishment, to be as American as any Texas G.I. And I found my experience was shared by every American writer I knew in Paris. Like me, they had been divorced from their origins, and it turned out to make very little difference that the origins of white Americans were European and mine were African — they were no more at home in Europe than I was.

The fact that I was the son of a slave and they were the sons of free men meant less, by the time we confronted each other on European soil, than the fact that we were both searching for our separate identities. When we had found these, we seemed to be saying, why, then, we would no longer need to cling to the shame and bitterness which had divided us so long.

It became terribly clear in Europe, as it never had been here, that we knew more about each other than any European ever could. And it also became clear that, no matter where our fathers had been born, or what they had endured, the fact of Europe had formed us both, was part of our identity and part of our inheritance.

I had been in Paris a couple of years before any of this became clear to me. When it did, I, like many a writer before me upon the discovery that his props have all been knocked out from under him, suffered a species of breakdown and was carried off to the mountains of Switzerland. There, in that absolutely alabaster landscape, armed with two Bessie Smith records and a typewriter, I began to try to re-create the life that I had first known as a child and from which I had spent so many years in flight.

It was Bessie Smith, through her tone and her cadence, who helped me to dig back to the way I myself must have spoken when I was a pickaninny, and to remember the things I had heard and seen and felt. I had buried them very deep. I had never listened to Bessie Smith in America (in the same way that, for years, I would not touch watermelon), but in Europe she helped to reconcile me to being a "nigger."

I do not think that I could have made this reconciliation here. Once I was able to accept my role — as distinguished, I must say, from my "place" — in the extraordinary drama which is America, I was released from the illusion that I hated America.

The story of what can happen to an American Negro writer in Europe simply illustrates, in some relief, what can happen to any American writer there. It is not meant, of course, to imply that it happens to them all, for Europe can be very crippling, too; and, anyway, a writer, when he has made his first breakthrough, has simply won a crucial skirmish in a dangerous, unending and unpredictable battle. Still, the breakthrough is important, and the point is that an American writer, in order to achieve it, very often has to leave this country.

The American writer, in Europe, is released, first of all, from the necessity of apologizing for himself. It is not until he *is* released from the habit of flexing his muscles and proving that he is just a "regular guy" that he realizes how crippling this habit has been. It is not necessary for him, there, to pretend to be something he is not, for the artist does not encounter in Europe the same suspicion he encounters here. Whatever the Europeans may actually think of artists, they have killed enough of them off by now to know that they are as real — and as persistent — as rain, snow, taxes or businessmen.

Of course, the reason for Europe's comparative clarity concerning the different functions of men in society is that European society has always been divided into classes in a way that American society never has been. A European writer considers himself to be part of an old and honorable tradition — of intellectual activity, of letters — and his choice of a vocation does not cause him any uneasy wonder as to whether or not it will cost him all his friends. But this tradition does not exist in America.

On the contrary, we have a very deep-seated distrust of real intellectual effort (probably because we suspect that it will destroy, as I hope it does, that myth of America to which we cling so desperately). An American writer fights his way to one of the lowest rungs on the American social ladder by means of pure bull-headedness and an indescribable series of odd jobs. He probably *has* been a "regular fellow" for much of his adult life, and it is not easy for him to step out of that lukewarm bath.

We must, however, consider a rather serious paradox: though American society is more mobile than Europe's, it is easier to cut across social and occupational lines there than it is here. This has something to do, I think, with the problem of status in American life. Where everyone has status, it is also perfectly possible, after all, that no one has. It seems inevitable, in any case, that a man may become uneasy as to just what his status is.

But Europeans have lived with the idea of status for a long time. A man can be as proud of being a good waiter as of being a good actor, and in neither case feel threatened. And this means that the actor and the waiter can have a freer and more genuinely friendly relationship in Europe than they are likely to have here. The waiter does not feel, with obscure resentment, that the actor has "made it," and the actor is not tormented by the fear that he may find himself, tomorrow, once again a waiter.

This lack of what may roughly be called social paranoia causes the American writer in Europe to feel — almost certainly for the first time in his life — that he can reach out to everyone, that he is accessible to everyone and open to everything. This is an extraordinary feeling. He feels, so to speak, his own weight, his own value.

It is as though he suddenly came out of a dark tunnel and found himself beneath the open sky. And, in fact, in Paris, I began to see the sky for what seemed to be the first time. It was borne in on me — and it did not make me feel melancholy — that this sky had been there before I was born and would be there when I was dead. And it was up to me, therefore, to make of my brief opportunity the most that could be made.

I was born in New York, but have lived only in pockets of it. In Paris, I lived in all parts of the city — on the Right Bank and the Left, among the bourgeoisie and among *les misérables*, and knew all kinds of people, from pimps and prostitutes in Pigalle to Egyptian bankers in Neuilly. This may sound extremely unprincipled or even obscurely immoral: I found it healthy. I love to talk to people, all kinds of people, and almost everyone, as I hope we still know, loves a man who loves to listen.

This perpetual dealing with people very different from myself caused a shattering in me of preconceptions I scarcely knew I held. The writer is meeting in Europe people who are not American, whose sense of reality is entirely different from his own. They may love or hate or admire or fear or envy this country — they see it, in any case, from another point of view, and this forces the writer to reconsider many things he had always taken for granted. This reassessment, which can be very painful, is also very valuable.

This freedom, like all freedom, has its dangers and its responsibilities. One day it begins to be borne in on the writer, and with great force, that he is living in Europe as an American. If he were living there as a European, he would be living on a different and far less attractive continent.

This crucial day may be the day on which an Algerian taxi-driver tells him how it feels to be an Algerian in Paris. It may be the day on which he passes a café terrace and catches a glimpse of the tense, intelligent and troubled face of Albert Camus. Or it may be the day on which someone asks him to explain Little Rock and he begins to feel that it would be simpler — and, corny as the words may sound, more honorable — to *go* to Little Rock than sit in Europe, on an American passport, trying to explain it.

This is a personal day, a terrible day, the day to which his entire sojourn has been tending. It is the day he realizes that there are no untroubled countries in this fearfully troubled world; that if he has been preparing himself for anything in Europe, he has been preparing himself — for America. In short, the freedom that the American writer finds in Europe brings him, full circle, back to himself, with the responsibility for his development where it always was: in his own hands.

Even the most incorrigible maverick has to be born somewhere. He may leave the group that produced him — he may be forced to — but nothing will efface his origins, the marks of which he carries with him everywhere. I think it is important to know this and even find it a matter for rejoicing, as the strongest people do, regardless of their station. On this acceptance, literally, the life of a writer depends.

The charge has often been made against American writers that they do not describe society, and have no interest in it. They only describe individuals in opposition to it, or isolated from it. Of course, what the American writer is describing is his own situation. But what is *Anna Karenina* describing if not the tragic fate of the isolated individual, at odds with her time and place?

The real difference is that Tolstoy was describing an old and dense society in which everything seemed — to the people in it, though not to Tolstoy — to be fixed forever. And the book is a masterpiece because Tolstoy was able to fathom, and make us see, the hidden laws which really governed this society and made Anna's doom inevitable.

American writers do not have a fixed society to describe. The only society they know is one in which nothing is fixed and in which the individual must fight for his identity. This is a rich confusion, indeed, and it creates for the American writer unprecedented opportunities.

That the tensions of American life, as well as the possibilities, are tremendous is certainly not even a question. But these are dealt with in contemporary literature mainly compulsively; that is, the book is more likely to be a symptom of our tension than an examination of it. The time has come, God knows, for us to examine ourselves, but we can only do this if we are willing to free ourselves of the myth of America and try to find out what is really happening here.

Every society is really governed by hidden laws, by unspoken but profound assumptions on the part of the people, and ours is no exception. It is up to the American writer to find out what these laws and assumptions are. In a society much given to smashing taboos without thereby managing to be liberated from them, it will be no easy matter.

It is no wonder, in the meantime, that the American writer keeps running off to Europe. He needs sustenance for his journey and the best models he can find. Europe has what we do not have yet, a sense of the mysterious and inexorable limits of life, a sense, in a word, of tragedy. And we have what they sorely need: a new sense of life's possibilities.

In this endeavor to wed the vision of the Old World with that of the New, it is the writer, not the statesman, who is our strongest arm. Though we do not wholly believe it yet, the interior life is a real life, and the intangible dreams of people have a tangible effect on the world.

John O. Killens (1916-   )

The Black Psyche

Born in Macon, Georgia, John O. Killens studied law at Columbia University and at New York University. He has worked with the National Labor Relations Board, and presently is a writer-in-residence at Fisk University.

Best known for his novels — *Youngblood* (1954), *And Then We Heard the Thunder* (1964), and *'Sippi* (1967), Killens insists that the black writer has the responsibility to search for his subject matter within the experiences of his race and to present those experiences with full consciousness of his racial identity. In other words, a black writer is not merely a writer who is black; instead, he is a black man who is a writer.

The title of Killens's collection of essays is, of course, an ironic reversal of the philosophy by which white colonials justified their subjugation of dark-skinned people. They argued that it was the white man's burden to advise and provide for dark-skinned natives, who, incapable of directing their own destiny, would not survive without such assistance. Rejecting paternalistic philosophy, Killens examines interracial relationships in language and style which frequently suggest a deliberate rejection of the traditional formal literary idiom.

The Black Psyche

When I was a boy in Macon, Georgia, one of the greatest compliments a benevolent white man could give a Negro was usually found in the obituary column of the local newspaper: "He was a black man, but he had a white heart." And the burden of every black man was supposedly just a little easier to bear that day. It was a time when many of us black folk laughed at the antics of *Amos 'n' Andy* and wept copious tears at a ridiculous movie very aptly titled *Imitation of Life*. Most of us looked at life through the eyes of white America.

The great fictional (and film) masterpieces on the American racial theme usually fell into two categories. One theme dealt with the utter heartbreak of the mulatto, who rejected his black blood and was in turn rejected by his white blood. A variation of this theme was the shattering experience of "passing." The other theme was the "Uncle Tom," or what I prefer to call the "Gunga Din," theme. This one also had many variations, but over all there was the image created by that great apologist for colonialism, Rudyard Kipling, of a man who

> *. . . For all 'is dirty 'ide*
> *'E was white, clear white, inside*
> *When 'e went to tend the wounded*
> *under fire!*

With some "additional touches" by Hollywood, dear old "white inside" Gunga evolved as a marvelous figment of Western man's wistful imagination, the personification of his wish fulfillment. Remember Gunga? He was a water boy for the British regiment and in the movie version, finally blew the bugle against his own people. And how "whiter" inside could a "noble savage" be?

I am waging a quiet little campaign at the moment to substitute the term "Gunga Din" for that much maligned character "Uncle Tom" in designating the contemporary water boys who still blow the bugles for old Massa. For although Mrs. Stowe's beloved "Uncle Tom" was indeed an Uncle Tom, as we understand the term today, he nevertheless, in the final confrontation, chose death rather than blow the whistle on his people.

Variations of the Gunga Din theme were seen in a rash of movie epics, like *Gone with the Wind* and *Virginia* and *Kentucky*, etc., ad infinitum, *ad nauseam*, always played magnificently with tongue in cheek by such stalwarts as Hattie McDaniel and Louise Beavers. In the great emotional scene the black "mammy" was usually in the big house, weeping and moaning over little pure-white-as-the-driven-snow Missy Anne, who had just sneezed, while Mammy's own young-un was dying of double pneumonia, unattended, down in the cabins. All in all, the slaves were presented as carefree and contented in their idyllic degradation. If the black man really believed in this romantic version of American slavery, he would have long since wasted away, pining for those good old happy-go-lucky days of bondage.

Last year I did considerable research on that bygone "utopian" era, and I got a very different picture, slightly less romantic. I found that the slaves were so happy that most of the plantation owners couldn't afford the astronomical rates of fire insurance. These rapturous slaves kept setting fire to the cotton patches, burning down the plantation, every day the good Lord sent them. They organized countless insurrections, killed their masters, poisoned their mistresses, even put spiders in the Big House soup. They demonstrated their contentment in most peculiar ways.

The point is, most white Americans cling desperately to these wish-fulfillment fantasies, but most of us Negroes have become unbelievers. We don't break into cheers any more when the cowboys chase the Indians across the movie screen, or when the Army finally captures old John Brown. Indeed, our favorite epic of the west has become Custer's Last Stand. Sitting Bull is a colored hero. Many black folk wish that this mighty warrior had been an American Negro.

I shall never forget an evening I spent in a movie house in Hollywood watching the closed-circuit television broadcast of the first Patterson-Johannson fight, and the great shame I felt for my white countrymen that night as they began to sense a possible victory for the white foreigner over the black American. Forgotten entirely was the fact that softhearted Floyd Patterson was fellow countryman. Color superseded patriotism. As I sat there hearing shouted exhortations, like "Kill the nigger!", I felt that Patterson and I were aliens in a strange and hostile country, and that Ingemar was at home among his people. In fairness to my countrymen in the closed circuits of America that night, their reactions were not intellectual, not even willful. They were spontaneous, not unlike a conditioned reflex. This ecstasy at the sudden emergence of a new white hope came from their hearts, their souls, their bellies. It was their white insides reacting.

I have been told that this incident had no racial implications at all, that these rabid Johannson fans were merely upholding the old American tradition of rooting for the underdog. Well, I was also rooting for the underdog, and I knew that, win or lose, the underdog in America was Floyd Patterson, Harry Belafonte, Emmett Till, Rosa Parks, Meredith, Poitier, the black American, I, *me*. The words "Kill the nigger!" could not possibly have come screaming from my throat, subconsciously, unconsciously, or otherwise. Nor could they from any other black man's throat.

Just as surely as East is East and West is West, there is a "black" psyche in America and there is a "white" one, and the sooner we face up to this psychological, social, and cultural reality, the sooner the twain shall meet. Our emotional chemistry is different from white America's. Your joy is very often our anger, and your despair our hope. Most of us came here in chains, and many of you came here to escape your chains. Your freedom was our slavery, and therein lies the bitter difference in the way we look at life. You created the myth of the faithful slave, but we know that the "loyal slave" is a contradiction in terms. We understand, though, that the master must always make himself believe in the undying love of his slave.

Ironically enough, the fathers of our magnificent Revolution, Washington and Jefferson, themselves owned hundreds of human chattels, and even though the great Thomas Jefferson made many speeches against the peculiar institution, he was never able to convince himself to the extent of manumitting his own slaves during his lifetime. Surely the great irony of the situation did not escape my ancestors back in the days of the Revolution. And now, today, it does not escape their great-great-grandchildren. When we hear some white statesman use the phrase "the Free World," even though the same white statesman may very well be the Governor of the State of Mississippi or Alabama, or even President of these United States, for that matter, we — as the slaves of Washington and Jefferson must have done — stare at him incredulously and cannot believe our ears. And we wonder how this word "freedom" can have such vastly different meanings, such conflicting connotations.

But the time has come for you (white America) and me (black America) to work this thing out once and for all, to examine and evaluate the differences between us and the differences inside us. Time is swiftly running out, and a new dialogue is indispensable. It is so long overdue it is already half past midnight.

And let us be clear on one thing. My fight is not to be a white man in a black skin, but to inject some black blood, some black intelligence, some black humaneness, into the pallid mainstream of American life — culturally, socially, psychologically, philosophically. This is the truer, deeper meaning of the Negro revolt which is not yet a revolution — to get America ready for the middle of the twentieth century, which is already magnificently here.

This new epoch has caught our country (yours and mine) dozing in a sweet nostalgia of the good old days. Our country slumbers in a world of yesteryears, before Africa and Asia got up off their knees and threw off the black man's burden. The good old days when you threw pennies to the "natives." And there were gunboats in the China Sea and Big Stick policies and Monroe Doctrines and "Gold Coasters" from the U.K. sipped their gin-and-tonics in Accra and Lagos and talked about the "natives," as they basked in their roles of Great White Fathers in that best of all possible worlds.

That world is gone forever, and black and brown men everywhere are glad, deep in their hearts, though most Western men are chagrined, which may be the understatement of the century. The title of the great Duke Ellington's song has come true: "Things Ain't What They Used to Be." And the good news, or the bad news, depending on your point of view, is: Things ain't never going to be anything like they used to be. This is why the world is becoming too much for Western men, however liberal, even some radical Western men, whoever you are, and wherever. But the world is becoming more and more to my liking, to my taste and in my image. It gladdens my heart to see black and brown men and women walk with dignity in the United Nations, in affirmation of the manhood and the selfhood of the entire human race.

The American Negro, you see, is an Anglo-Saxon invention, a role the Anglo-Saxon gentleman created for the black man in this drama known euphemistically as the American Way of Life. It began as an economic expedient, frankly, because you wanted somebody to work for nothing. It is still that, but now it is much more than that. It has become a way of life within a way of life, socially, economically, psychologically, philosophically. The Negro Invention, hatched in the brave New World, ultimately and rapidly became a rationalization for the colonializing of three-quarters of the earth's peoples. All non-whites throughout the world became "niggers" and therefore proper material for "civilizing" and "Christianizing" (cruel euphemisms for colonization, exploitation, genocide, and slavery).

And now, in the middle of the twentieth century, I, the Negro, like my counterparts in Asia and Africa and South America and on the islands of the many seas, am refusing to be your "nigger" any longer. Even some of us "favored," "talented," "unusual," ones are refusing to be your educated, sophisticated, split-leveled "niggers" any more. We refuse to look at ourselves through the eyes of white America.

We are not fighting for the right to be like you. We respect ourselves too much for that. When we advocate freedom, we mean freedom for us to be black, or brown, and you to be white and yet live together in a free and equal society. This is the only way that integration can bring dignity for both of us. I, for one, am growing weary of those well-meaning white liberals who are forever telling me they don't know what color I am. The very fact that they always single me out at every cocktail party to gratuitously make me the beneficiary of their blessed assurances gives the lie to their pronouncements.

My fight is not for racial sameness but for racial equality and against racial prejudice and discrimination. I work for the day when black people will be free of the racist pressures to be white like you; a day when "good hair" and "high yaller" and bleaching cream and hair straighteners will be obsolete. What a tiresome place America would be if freedom meant we all had to think alike or be the same color or wear that same gray flannel suit! That road leads to the conformity of the graveyard.

If relationships are to improve between us Americans, black and white and otherwise, if the country is to be changed and saved, we will have to face up to the fact that differences do exist between us. All men react to life through man-made symbols. Even our symbolic reactions are different from yours. To give a few examples:

In the center of a little Southern town near the border of Mississippi there is a water tower atop which sits a large white cross, illumined at night with a lovely (awesome to Negroes) neon brightness, which can be seen for miles. To most white Americans, seeing it for the first time, it is a beacon that symbolizes the Cross upon which Jesus died, and it gives them a warm feeling. But it puts an angry knot in a black man's belly. To him it symbolizes the very "Christian" K.K.K. Just as to the average white man, a courthouse, even in Mississippi, is a place where justice is dispensed. Yet to me, the black man, it is a place where justice is dispensed with.

We even have a different historical perspective. Most white Americans, even today, look upon the Reconstruction period as a horrible time of "carpetbagging," and "black politicians," and "black corruption," the absolutely lowest ebb in the Great American Story. Oh, the oceans of bitter tears American writers have wept for that ill-begotten era. Oh, the shame of it all, the way those Southern patriots were treated after that unfortunate war, that horrendous misunderstanding.

We black folk, however, look upon Reconstruction as the most democratic period in the history of this nation; a time when the dream the founders dreamed was almost within reach and right there for the taking; a time of democratic fervor the like of which was never seen before and never since. For all we know, it was a time when America could have won the world but lost it, probably forever. We don't share your feeling that the Negro was not ready for the franchise. We think that the first slaves on that first slave ship were men and women and therefore capable of being citizens anywhere. This is our understanding of democracy. We are not impressed with the mess white Americans (educated and illiterate ones) have made of this Republic, and apparently, because of their whiteness, they were born ready. Apparently, they were endowed by "their creator."

For us, Reconstruction was the time when two black men were Senators in the Congress of the United States from the State of Mississippi; when black men served in the legislatures of all the states in Dixie; and when those "corrupt" legislatures gave to the South its first public-school education. And the lowest ebb for us black folk came on the heels of the Great Betrayal, when the government in Washington turned us over to the benevolent Ku Klux Klan and the Knights of the Camellias.

Nor do we share your romantic view of Rob Lee and Jeff Davis. Certainly, to most of us who have thought about the matter, they were traitors, pure and simple. We put them in the same inglorious category as the infamous Benedict Arnold.

I shall never forget the feeling I had one morning in the fall of 1957, in a Hollywood hotel, when I awoke and tuned into the outside world of television. There before my eyes were American soldiers, black and white, rolling into Little Rock, Arkansas, with their rifles at the ready. I cried that morning. I unashamedly wept. Wept for the moment that had been so long in the coming, the moment when for the first time in my life I felt that the nation gave a damn about *me*. One courageous black woman and eight innocent beautiful black children had laid down the gauntlet and brought the nation to the brink of human decency.

Whatever the political considerations that dictated the move, I felt that the nation had committed itself again, in a way it had not done since Reconstruction. When I saw the Star-Spangled Banners waving from those jeeps and tanks as they rolled endlessly into Little Rock that morning, Old Glory meant more to me, the black American, *me*, than ever before in my life's brief span, including the forty-one months I spent in the service of my country during World War II. Oh yes, we black folk find it difficult to understand the nation's hesitation about sending troops to Mississippi to guarantee free elections when we read of American boys dying thousands of miles from home to ensure freedom for the Vietnamese. The subtlety escapes us.

Even our white hero symbols are different from yours. You give us moody Abe Lincoln, but many of us prefer John Brown, whom most of you hold in contempt as a fanatic; meaning, of course, that the firm dedication of any white man to the freedom of the black man is *prima-facie* evidence of perversion or insanity.

You look upon these times as the Atomic Age, the Space Age, the Cold War Era. But I believe that when the history of our times is written, it will not be so important who reached the moon first or who made the largest bomb. I believe the great significance will be that this was the century when most of mankind achieved freedom and human dignity, the age when racial prejudices became obsolete. For me, this is the Freedom Century.

So now it is time for you to understand us, because it is becoming increasingly hazardous for you not to. Dangerous for both of us. As Richard Wright said in his *Twelve Million Black Voices*, voices you chose not to heed: "Each day when you see us black folk upon the dusty land of your farms or upon the hard pavement of your city streets, you usually take us for granted and think you know us, but our history is far stranger than you suspect, and we are not what we seem." The Rev. Ralph Abernathy of Montgomery put it more humorously when he said that the new Negro of Montgomery had stopped laughing when he wasn't tickled and scratching when he didn't itch.

At the turn of the century, Negro prophet William Edward Burghardt DuBois warned the Western world: "The problem of the twentieth century is the problem of the color line." But who listens to a black prophet at such a time of endless frontiers for the white pioneers and missionaries? Now, in the middle of that same century, we are bringing down the curtain on this role you cast us in, and we will no longer be a party to our own degradation. We have become unbelievers, no longer believing in the absolute superiority of the white man's juju. You have never practiced what you preached. Why should we believe in you? Why would we want to be like you?

Yes, we are different from you and we are not invisible men, Ralph Ellison notwithstanding. We are the most visible of Americans.

Last spring, Charles Harris, Negro editor for Doubleday, and I had drinks at the Playboy Club in New York. We were so visible, everybody who came into the place stared at us more than they did the semi-naked bunnies. "Who're they? Ralph Bunche and Sonny Liston, or Joe Louis and Sammy Davis, Junior? Or maybe Willie Mays and Martin Luther King?" Oh yes, we have a very high degree of visibility.

But white Americans are great pretenders. Millions of you wish we were invisible, and so you make believe we are. You'd like to wish us out of existence so that the whole world would not see us, because our very life in this country, as black people, gives the lie before the world to your protestations of freedom and human brotherhood. The white man's juju is powerful stuff, but it cannot wish the Negro into invisibility. So you try the next best thing, pretending you can't tell one of us from the other.

The point is: Since we no longer look at ourselves through *your* eyes, our visibility, to *your* eyes, is a total irrelevance, to *us*. We no longer look to you for our identity. But this self-delusion on *your* part (that you don't see us and that you can't tell us one from the other) is dangerous for you and for *our* country. You always knew the difference between the "field" slave and the "house" one; between the "bad nigger" and the "good" one; between Gunga Din and old Nat Turner, between Dubois and Booker Washington.

In the summer and fall of 1961 I traveled in a Land Rover 12,000 miles through Africa. I talked to people in the cities, on the farms, in the villages. I talked with workers, farmers, artists, market women, ministers of state, politicians, teachers, and the same question was asked me everywhere I went: "How can we believe your country's professions of good will to us, with whom they have not lived, when they deny human dignity to you who come from us and have lived with them for centuries and helped to build their great civilization?"

It is a question that America has to answer to the entire New World of Africa and Asia. The only way we Americans, black and white, can answer it affirmatively is to make freedom and democracy work at home, here and now. Most Negroes still believe that the ultimate solution for us is in America, and I am as firmly convinced that the ultimate salvation of America is in the Negro.

The Negro loves America enough to criticize her fundamentally. Most white Americans simply can't be bothered. Ironically enough, in the middle of the twentieth century, the Negro is the new white hope. To live castrated in a great white harem and yet somehow maintain our black manhood and humanity — this is the essence of the new man created out of the Negro Invention. History may render the verdict that this was the greatest legacy handed to the New World by the West.

There are glaring exceptions to every rule, but it is a truism that American Negroes are the only people in America who, as a people, are for change. This is true, again, not innately because of our color, but because of what America made of our color. The *status quo* has ever been the bane of black existence.

We black folk have learned many lessons during our sojourn in this place. One of them is the truth of the Ghana proverb, "Only a fool points to his origin with his left hand." We are becoming prouder and prouder of our origins. And we know the profound difference between pride and arrogance; the difference, if you will, between James Meredith and Ross Barnett, both of Mississippi. Our dialogue will not be protest but affirmation of the human dignity of all people everywhere. Yes, our aim is to create a dialogue in full vindication of every lonesome disinherited "nigger," every black and brown man born of woman who ever dwelt upon this alien earth, which means, of course, that all mankind would be vindicated regardless of race, color, or religion. Our dialogue is anti-racist.

Sure, I know that there are white folk who want America to be the land of the free and home of the brave, but there are far too few of them, and many of them are rarely brave. I cherish old John Brown and Garrison and William Moore and Mike Schwerner and Andy Goodman and all the other winter soldiers. Let the winter patriots increase their ranks. Let those who truly love America join the valiant Negro Revolt and change and save our country.

LeRoi Jones (1934-   )

City of Harlem *and* Cold, Hurt, and Sorrow (Streets of Despair)

LeRoi Jones has become a spokesman and a leader for many young black people who are rebelling against traditions of society and art. Born in Newark, New Jersey, he attended the Newark branch of Rutgers University before transferring to Howard to complete his undergraduate education. After serving in the Army Air Force, Jones returned to civilian life as a teacher and a writer.

Jones first attracted attention with *Preface to a Twenty-Volume Suicide Note* (1961), a volume of poems which exhibited his talent in vigorous language and powerful imagery. Since that time, Jones has become increasingly controversial. His interpretation of the history of black people through their experience — *Blues People* — is a persuasive one. His plays — *Dutchman, The Slave, The Baptism, The Toilet* — have created sensation either because of their language or their thought. His most recent collection, *Tales* (1967), mingles sketches, essays, stories in what some young writers believe to be a significant and successful experiment to achieve greater flexibility for the short-story form.

The following selections from *Home* summarize the history of Harlem and sing its blues.

City of Harlem

In a very real sense, Harlem is the capital of Black America. And America has always been divided into black and white, and the

131

substance of the division is social, economic, and cultural. But even the name Harlem, now, means simply Negroes (even though some other peoples live there too). The identification is international as well: even in Belize, the capital of predominantly Negro British Honduras, there are vendors who decorate their carts with flowers and the names or pictures of Negro culture heroes associated with Harlem like Sugar Ray Robinson. Some of the vendors even wear t-shirts that say "Harlem, U.S.A." and they speak about it as a black Paris. In Havana a young Afro-Cuban begged me to tell him about the "big leg ladies" of Lenox Avenue, hoping, too, that I could provide some way for him to get to that mystic and romantic place.

There are, I suppose, contained within the central mythology of Harlem, almost as many versions of its glamour, and its despair, as there are places with people to make them up. (In one meaning of the name, Harlem is simply a place white cab drivers will not go.) And Harlem means not only Negroes, but, of course, whatever other associations one might connect with them. So in one breath Harlem will be the pleasure-happy center of the universe, full of loud, hippy mamas in electric colors and their fast, slick-head papas, all of them twisting and grinning in the streets in a kind of existential joyousness that never permits of sadness or responsibility. But in another breath this same place will be the gathering place for every crippling human vice, and the black men there simply victims of their own peculiar kind of sloth and childishness. But perhaps these are not such different versions after all; chances are both these stereotypes come from the same kinds of minds.

But Harlem, as it is, as it exists for its people, as an actual place where actual humans live — that is a very different thing. Though, to be sure, Harlem is a place — a city really — where almost anything any person could think of to say goes on, probably does go on, or has gone on, but like any other city, it must escape *any* blank generalization simply because it is alive, and changing each second with each breath any of its citizens take.

When Africans first got to New York, or New Amsterdam as the Dutch called it, they lived in the farthest downtown portions of the city, near what is now called The Bowery. Later, they shifted, and were shifted, as their numbers grew, to the section known as Greenwich Village. The Civil War Draft Riots in 1863 accounted for the next move by New York's growing Negro population.

After this violence (a few million dollars' worth of property was destroyed, and a Negro orphanage was burned to the ground) a great many Negroes moved across the river into Brooklyn. But many others moved farther uptown to an area just above what was known as Hell's Kitchen. The new Negro ghetto was known as Black Bohemia, and later, after the success of an all black regiment in the Spanish-American war, this section was called San Juan Hill. And even in the twenties when most Negroes had made their move even further uptown to Harlem, San Juan Hill was still a teeming branch office of black night life.

Three sections along the east side of Manhattan, The Tenderloin, Black Bohemia, and San Juan Hill or The Jungle featured all kinds of "sporting houses," cabarets, "dancing classes," afterhours gin mills, as well as the Gumbo Suppers, Fish Fries, Egg Nog Parties, Chitterlin' Struts, and Pigfoot Hops, before the Negroes moved still farther uptown.

The actual move into what is now Harlem was caused by quite a few factors, but there are a few that were particularly important as catalysts. First, locally, there were more race riots around the turn of the century between the white poor (as always) and the Negroes. Also, the Black Bohemia section was by now extremely overcrowded, swelled as it was by the influx of Negroes from all over the city. The section was a notorious red light district (but then there have only been two occupations a black woman could go into in America without too much trouble: the other was domestic help) and the overcrowding made worse by the moral squalor that poverty encourages meant that the growing local black population had to go somewhere. The imigrant groups living on both sides of the black ghetto fought in the streets to keep their own ghettos autonomous and pure, and the Negro had to go elsewhere.

At this time, just about the turn of the century, Harlem (an area which the first Africans had helped connect with the rest of the Dutch city by clearing a narrow road — Broadway — up into the woods of Nieuw Haarlem) was still a kind of semi-suburban area, populated, for the most part, by many of the city's wealthiest families. The elaborate estates of the eighteenth century, built by men like Alexander Hamilton and Roger Morris, were still being lived in, but by the descendants of wealthy merchants. (The Hamilton house still stands near Morningside Heights, as an historic landmark called The Grange. The Morris house, which was once lived in by Aaron Burr, is known as The Jumel House, and it still stands at the northern part of Harlem, near the Polo Grounds, as a museum run by the D.A.R. George Washington used it as his headquarters for a while during the Revolutionary War.) So there was still the quiet elegance of the nineteenth century brownstones and spacious apartment buildings, the wide drives, rolling greens, and huge-trunked trees.

What made the area open up to Negroes was the progress that America has always been proud of — an elevated railway went up in the nineties, and the very rich left immediately and the near rich very soon after. Saint Philips Church, after having its old site bought up by a railroad company, bought a large piece of property, with large apartment buildings, in the center of Harlem, and, baby, the panic was on. Rich and famous Negroes moved into the vacated luxury houses very soon after, including the area now known as "Strivers Row," which was made up of almost one hundred brick mansions designed by Stanford White. The panic was definitely on — but still only locally.

What really turned that quiet suburb into "Black Paris," was the coming of the First World War and the mass exodus of Negroes from the South to large urban centers. At the turn of the century most Negroes still lived in the South and were agricultural laborers, but the entrance of America into the War, and the desperate call for cheap unskilled labor, served to start thousands of Negroes scrambling North. The flow of immigrants from Europe had all but ceased by 1914, and the industrialists knew immediately where to turn. They even sent recruiters down into the South to entice the Negroes north. In 1900 the Negro population of New York City was 60,000; by 1920 it was 152,467; by 1930 it was 327,706. And most of these moved, of course, uptown.

It was this mass exodus during the early part of the century that was responsible for most of the black cities of the North — the huge Negro sections of New York, Chicago, Philadelphia, Detroit, etc. It was also responsible for what these sections would very shortly become, as the masses of Southern Negroes piled into their new Jordans, thinking to have a go at an innocent America.

The twenties are legend because they mark America's sudden insane entrance into the 20th century. The war had brought about a certain internationalism and prosperity (even, relatively speaking, for Negroes). During the twenties Harlem was the mecca of the good time and in many ways even came to symbolize the era called the Jazz Age. Delirious white people made the trip uptown to hear Negro musicians and singers, and watch Negro dancers, and even Negro intellectuals. It was, I suppose, the black man's debut into the most sophisticated part of America. The old darkies of the plantation were suddenly all over the North, and making a whole lot of noise.

There were nightclubs in Harlem that catered only to white audiences, but with the best Negro entertainers. White intellectuals made frequent trips to Harlem, not only to find out about a newly emerging black America, but to party with an international set of swinging bodies. It was the era of Ellington at The Cotton Club for the sensual, and The New Negro for the intellectual. Everyone spoke optimistically of the Negro Renaissance, and The New Negro, as if, somehow, the old Negro wasn't good enough. Harlem sparkled then, at least externally, and it took the depression to dull that sparkle, and the long lines of unemployed Negroes and the longer lines at the soup kitchens and bread queues brought reality down hard on old and new Negroes alike. So the tourist trade diminished, and colorful Harlem became just a social liability for the white man, and an open air jail for the black.

The cold depression thirties, coupled with the decay of old buildings and ancient neighborhoods, and, of course, the seeming inability of the "free enterprise" system to provide either jobs or hope for a great many black people in the city of Harlem, have served to make this city another kind of symbol. For many Negroes, whether they live in Harlem or not, the city is simply a symbol of naked oppression. You can walk along 125th Street any evening and meet about one hundred uniformed policemen, who are there, someone will tell you, to protect the people from themselves.

For many Negroes Harlem is a place one escapes from, and lives in shame about for the rest of his life. But this is one of the weirdest things about the American experience, that it can oppress a man, almost suck his life away, and then make him so ashamed that he was among the oppressed rather than the oppressors, that he will never offer any protest.

The legitimate cultural tradition of the Negro in Harlem (and America) is one of wild happiness, usually at some black man's own invention — of speech, of dress, of gait, the sudden twist of a musical phrase, the warmness or hurt of someone's voice. But that culture is also one of hatred and despair. Harlem must contain all of this and be capable of producing all of these emotions.

People line the streets in summer — on the corners or hanging out the windows — or head for other streets in winter. Vendors go by slowly . . . and crowds of people from movies or church. (Saturday afternoons, warm or cold, 125th is jammed with shoppers and walkers, and the record stores scream through loudspeakers at the

street.) Young girls, doctors, pimps, detectives, preachers, drum-
mers, accountants, gamblers, labor organizers, postmen, wives,
Muslims, junkies, the employed, and the unemployed: all going
someplace — an endless stream of Americans, whose singularity in
America is that they are black and can never honestly enter into
the lunatic asylum of white America.

Harlem for this reason is a community of nonconformists, since
any black American, simply by virtue of his blackness, is weird, a
nonconformist in this society. A community of nonconformists, not
an artists' colony — though blind "ministers" still wander sometimes along 137th Street, whispering along the strings of their
guitars — but a colony of old-line Americans, who can hold out,
even if it is a great deal of the time in misery and ignorance, but
still hold out, against the hypocrisy and sterility of big-time
America, and still try to make their own lives, simply because of
their color, but by now, not so simply, because that color now does
serve to identify people in America whose feelings about it are
not broadcast every day on television.

Cold, Hurt, and Sorrow (Streets of Despair)

These streets stretch from one end of America to the other and
connect like a maze from which very few can fully escape. Despair
sits on this country in most places like a charm, but there is a
special gray death that loiters in the streets of an urban Negro
slum. And the men who walk those streets, tracing and retracing
their steps to some hopeless job or a pitiful rooming house or
apartment or furnished room, sometimes stagger under the weight
of that gray, humiliated because it is not even "real."

Sometimes walking along among the ruined shacks and lives of
the worst Harlem slum, there is a feeling that just around the
corner you'll find yourself in South Chicago or South Philadelphia,
maybe even Newark's Third Ward. In these places life, and its
possibility, has been distorted almost identically. And the distor-
tion is as old as its sources: the fear, frustration, and hatred that
Negroes have always been heir to in America. It is just that in the
cities, which were once the black man's twentieth century "Jor-
dan," *promise* is a dying bitch with rotting eyes. And the stink of
her dying is a deadly killing fume.

The blues singers know all this. They knew before they got to
the cities. "I'd rather drink muddy water, sleep in a hollow log,

than be in New York City treated like a dirty dog." And when they arrived, in those various cities, it was much worse than even they had imagined. The city blues singers are still running all that down. Specifically, it's what a man once named for me unnatural adversity. It is social, it is economic, it is cultural and historical. Some of its products are emotional and psychological; some are even artistic, as if Negroes suffered better than anyone else. But it's hard enough to be a human being under any circumstances, but when there is an entire civilization determined to stop you from being one, things get a little more desperately complicated. What do you do then?

You can stand in doorways late nights and hit people in the head. You can go to church Saturday nights and Sundays and three or four times during the week. You can stick a needle in your arm four or five times a day, and bolster the economy. You can buy charms and herbs and roots, or wear your hat backwards to keep things from getting worse. You can drink till screaming is not loud enough, and the coldest night is all right to sleep outside in. You can buy a big car . . . if the deal goes down. There's so much, then, you can do, to yourself, or to somebody else. Another man sings, "I'm drinkin' t.n.t., I'm smokin dynamite, I hope some screwball starts a fight."

One can never talk about Harlem in purely social terms, though there are ghetto facts that make any honest man shudder. It is the tone, the quality of suffering each man knows as his own that finally must be important, but this is the most difficult thing to get to. (There are about twenty young people from one small Southern town, all friends, all living within the same few blocks of the black city, all of whom are junkies, communally hooked. What kind of statistic is *that?* And what can you say when you read it?)

The old folks kept singing, there will be a better day . . . or, the sun's gonna shine in my back door some day . . . or, I've had my fun if I don't get well no more. What did they want? What would that sun turn out to be?

Hope is a delicate suffering. Its waste products vary, but most of them are meaningful. And as a cat named Mean William once said, can you be glad, if you've never been sad?

Eldridge Cleaver (1934-   )

The White Race and Its Heroes.

In prison Eldridge Cleaver wrote the essays of *Soul on Ice*, which has been praised by critics and scholars. Literary historian Maxwell Geismar wrote, "Cleaver's is one of the distinctive new literary voices to be heard." Kenneth Clark, a psychologist, praised "the explicit and implicit diagnoses of the moral dry rot which mocks our democracy." Novelist Norman Mailer wrote, "His style has the clarity and strength of someone talking to you about a subject he understands, a tone which very few writers ever achieve, no matter how long they've been working at it."

Born in Little Rock, Arkansas, Cleaver received his formal education in the black ghetto of Los Angeles. In prison, however, he gained a better education. There he did not merely learn to write more effectively than most people learn in sixteen years of formal education; more importantly, he learned to look deeply into individuals and society. His essays describe "the forces which shaped his life and which are currently molding our national destiny." Influenced first by the Muslims, Cleaver later rejected their philosophy of racial hatred to assume a position closer to that of Malcolm X.

In the following selection, Cleaver explores the psychological forces currently motivating the actions of young white people.

The White Race and Its Heroes

White people cannot, in the generality, be taken as models of how
to live. Rather, the white man is himself in sore need of new standards, which will release him from his confusion and place him once
again in fruitful communion with the depths of his own being.

> James Baldwin
> — *The Fire Next Time*

Right from the go, let me make one thing absolutely clear: I am
not now, nor have I ever been, a white man. Nor, I hasten to add,
am I now a Black Muslim — although I used to be. But I *am* an
Ofay Watcher, a member of that unchartered, amorphous league
which has members on all continents and the islands of the seas.
Ofay Watchers Anonymous, we might be called, because we exist
concealed in the shadows wherever colored people have known
oppression by whites, by white enslavers, colonizers, imperialists,
and neo-colonialists.

Did it irritate you, compatriot, for me to string those epithets
out like that? Tolerate me. My intention was not necessarily to
sprinkle salt over anyone's wounds. I did it primarily to relieve
a certain pressure on my brain. Do you cop that? If not, then we're
in trouble, because we Ofay Watchers have a pronounced tendency
to slip into that mood. If it is bothersome to you, it is quite a task
for me because not too long ago it was my way of life to preach, as
ardently as I could, that the white race is a race of devils, created
by their maker to do evil, and make evil appear as good; that the
white race is the natural, unchangeable enemy of the black man,
who is the original man, owner, maker, cream of the planet Earth;
that the white race was soon to be destroyed by Allah, and that
the black man would then inherit the earth, which has always, in
fact, been his.

I have, so to speak, washed my hands in the blood of the martyr,
Malcolm X, whose retreat from the precipice of madness created
new room for others to turn about in, and I am now caught up in
that tiny space, attempting a maneuver of my own. Having renounced the teachings of Elijah Muhammad, I find that a rebirth
does not follow automatically, of its own accord, that a void is left
in one's vision, and this void seeks constantly to obliterate itself by
pulling one back to one's former outlook. I have tried a tentative
compromise by adopting a select vocabulary, so that now when I
see the whites of *their* eyes, instead of saying "devil" or "beast"

I say "imperialist" or "colonialist," and everyone seems to be happier.

In silence, we have spent our years watching the ofays, trying to understand them, on the principle that you have a better chance coping with the known than with the unknown. Some of us have been, and some still are, interested in learning whether it is *ultimately* possible to live in the same territory with people who seem so disagreeable to live with; still others want to get as far away from ofays as possible. What we share in common is the desire to break the ofays' power over us.

At times of fundamental social change, such as the era in which we live, it is easy to be deceived by the onrush of events, beguiled by the craving for social stability into mistaking transitory phenomena for enduring reality. The strength and permanence of "white backlash" in America is just such an illusion. However much this rear-guard action might seem to grow in strength, the initiative, and the future, rest with those whites and blacks who have liberated themselves from the master/slave syndrome. And these are to be found mainly among the youth.

Over the past twelve years there has surfaced a political conflict between the generations that is deeper, even, than the struggle between the races. Its first dramatic manifestation was within the ranks of the Negro people, when college students in the South, fed up with Uncle Tom's hat-in-hand approach to revolution, threw off the yoke of the NAACP. When these students initiated the first sit-ins, their spirit spread like a raging fire across the nation, and the technique of non-violent direct action, constantly refined and honed into a sharp cutting tool, swiftly matured. The older Negro "leaders," who are now all die-hard advocates of this tactic, scolded the students for sitting-in. The students rained down contempt upon their hoary heads. In the pre-sit-in days, these conservative leaders had always succeeded in putting down insurgent elements among the Negro people. (A measure of their power, prior to the students' rebellion, is shown by their success in isolating such great black men as the late W. E. B. DuBois and Paul Robeson, when these stalwarts, refusing to bite their tongues, lost favor with the U.S. government by their unstinting efforts to link up the Negro revolution with national liberation movements around the world.)

The "Negro leaders," and the whites who depended upon them to control their people, were outraged by the impudence of the students. Calling for a moratorium on student initiative, they were greeted instead by an encore of sit-ins, and retired to their ivory towers to contemplate the new phenomenon. Others, less prudent because held on a tighter leash by the whites, had their careers brought to an abrupt end because they thought they could lead a black/white backlash against the students, only to find themselves in a kind of Bay of Pigs. Negro college presidents, who expelled students from all-Negro colleges in an attempt to quash the demonstrations, ended up losing their jobs; the victorious students would no longer allow them to preside over the campuses. The spontaneous protests on southern campuses over the repressive measures of their college administrations were an earnest of the Free Speech upheaval which years later was to shake the UC campus at Berkeley. In countless ways, the rebellion of the black students served as catalyst for the brewing revolt of the whites.

What has suddenly happened is that the white race has lost its heroes. Worse, its heroes have been revealed as villains and its greatest heroes as the arch-villains. The new generations of whites, appalled by the sanguine and despicable record carved over the face of the globe by their race in the last five hundred years, are rejecting the panoply of white heroes, whose heroism consisted in erecting the inglorious edifice of colonialism and imperialism; heroes whose careers rested on a system of foreign and domestic exploitation, rooted in the myth of white supremacy and the manifest destiny of the white race. The emerging shape of a new world order, and the requisites for survival in such a world, are fostering in young whites a new outlook. They recoil in shame from the spectacle of cowboys and pioneers — their heroic forefathers whose exploits filled earlier generations with pride — galloping across a movie screen shooting down Indians like Coke bottles. Even Winston Churchill, who is looked upon by older whites as perhaps the greatest hero of the twentieth century — even he, because of the system of which he was a creature and which he served, is an arch-villain in the eyes of the young white rebels.

At the close of World War Two, national liberation movements in the colonized world picked up new momentum and audacity, seeking to cash in on the democratic promises made by the Allies during the war. The Atlantic Charter, signed by President Roosevelt and Prime Minister Churchill in 1941, affirming "the right of all people to choose the form of government under which they may live," established the principle, although it took years of postwar struggle to give this piece of rhetoric even the apperance of reality. And just as world revolution has prompted the oppressed to re-evaluate their self-image in terms of the changing conditions, to slough off the servile attitudes inculcated by long years of sub-ordination, the same dynamics of change have prompted the white people of the world to re-evaluate their self-image as well, to dis-abuse themselves of the Master Race psychology developed over centuries of imperial hegemony.

It is among the white youth of the world that the greatest change is taking place. It is they who are experiencing the great psychic pain of waking into consciousness to find their inherited heroes turned by events into villains. Communication and under-standing between the older and younger generations of whites has entered a crisis. The elders, who, in the tradition of privileged classes or races, genuinely do not understand the youth, trapped by old ways of thinking and blind to the future, have only just begun to be vexed — because the youth have only just begun to rebel. So thoroughgoing is the revolution in the psyches of white youth that the traditional tolerance which every older generation has found it necessary to display is quickly exhausted, leaving a gulf of fear, hostility, mutual misunderstanding, and contempt.

The rebellion of the oppressed peoples of the world, along with the Negro revolution in America, have opened the way to a new evaluation of history, re-examination of the role played by the white race since the beginning of European expansion. The positive achievements are also there in the record, and future generations will applaud them. But there can be no applause now, not while the master still holds the whip in his hand! Not even the master's own children can find it possible to applaud him — he cannot even applaud himself! The negative rings too loudly. Slave-catchers, slaveowners, murderers, butchers, invaders, oppressors — the white heroes have acquired new names. The great white statesmen whom school children are taught to revere are revealed as the architects of systems of human exploitation and slavery. Religious leaders are exposed as condoners and justifiers of all these evil deeds. Schoolteachers and college professors are seen as a clique of brainwashers and whitewashers.

The white youth of today are coming to see, intuitively, that to escape the onus of the history their fathers made they must face and admit the moral truth concerning the works of their fathers. That such venerated figures as George Washington and Thomas Jefferson owned hundreds of black slaves, that all of the Presidents up to Lincoln presided over a slave state, and that every President since Lincoln connived politically and cynically with the issues affecting the human rights and general welfare of the broad masses of the American people — these facts weigh heavily upon the hearts of these young people.

The elders do not like to give these youngsters credit for being able to understand what is going on and what has gone on. When speaking of juvenile delinquency, or the rebellious attitude of today's youth, the elders employ a glib rhetoric. They speak of the "alienation of youth," the desire of the young to be independent, the problems of "the father image" and "the mother image" and their effect upon growing children who lack sound models upon which to pattern themselves. But they consider it bad form to connect the problems of the youth with the central event of our era — the national liberation movements abroad and the Negro revolution at home. The foundations of authority have been blasted to bits in America because the whole society has been indicted, tried, and convicted of injustice. To the youth, the elders are Ugly Americans; to the elders, the youth have gone mad.

The rebellion of the white youth has gone through four broadly discernible stages. First there was an initial recoiling away, a rejection of the conformity which America expected, and had always received, sooner or later, from its youth. The disaffected youth were refusing to participate in the system, having discovered that America, far from helping the underdog, was up to its ears in the mud trying to hold the dog down. Because of the publicity and self-advertisements of the more vocal rebels, this period has come to be known as the beatnik era, although not all of the youth affected by these changes thought of themselves as beatniks. The howl of the beatniks and their scathing, outraged denunciation of the system — characterized by Ginsberg as Moloch, a bloodthirsty Semitic deity to which the ancient tribes sacrificed their firstborn children — was a serious, irrevocable declaration of war. It is revealing that the elders looked upon the beatniks as mere obscene misfits who were too lazy to take baths and too stingy to buy a haircut. The elders had eyes but couldn't see, ears but couldn't hear — not even when the message came through as clearly as in this remarkable passage from Jack Kerouac's *On the Road:*

> At lilac evening, I walked with every muscle aching among the lights of 27th and Welton in the Denver colored section, wishing I were a Negro, feeling that the best the white world had offered was not enough ecstasy for me, not enough life, joy, kicks, darkness, music, not enough night. I wished I were a Denver Mexican, or even

a poor overworked Jap, anything but what I so drearily was, a "white man" disillusioned. All my life I'd had white ambitions. . . . I passed the dark porches of Mexican and Negro homes; soft voices were there, occasionally the dusky knee of some mysterious sensuous gal; the dark faces of the men behind rose arbors. Little children sat like sages in ancient rocking chairs.

The second stage arrived when these young people, having decided emphatically that the world, and particularly the U.S.A., was unacceptable to them in its present form, began an active search for roles they could play in changing the society. If many of these young people were content to lay up in their cool beat pads, smoking pot and listening to jazz in a perpetual orgy of esoteric bliss, there were others, less crushed by the system, who recognized the need for positive action. Moloch could not ask for anything more than to have its disaffected victims withdrawn into safe, passive, apolitical little nonparticipatory islands, in an economy less and less able to provide jobs for the growing pool of unemployed. If all the unemployed had followed the lead of the beatniks, Moloch would gladly have legalized the use of euphoric drugs and marijuana, passed out free jazz albums and sleeping bags, to all those willing to sign affidavits promising to remain "beat." The non-beat disenchanted white youth were attracted magnetically to the Negro revolution, which had begun to take on a mass, insurrectionary tone. But they had difficulty understanding their relationship to the Negro, and what role "whites" could play in a "Negro revolution." For the time being they watched the Negro activists from afar.

The third stage, which is rapidly drawing to a close, emerged when white youth started joining Negro demonstrations in large numbers. The presence of whites among the demonstrators emboldened the Negro leaders and allowed them to use tactics they never would have been able to employ with all-black troops. The racist conscience of America is such that murder does not register as murder, really, unless the victim is white. And it was only when the newspapers and magazines started carrying pictures and stories of white demonstrators being beaten and maimed by mobs and police that the public began to protest. Negroes have become so used to this double standard that they, too, react differently to the death of a white. When white freedom riders were brutalized along with blacks, a sigh of relief went up from the black masses, because the blacks knew that white blood is the coin of freedom in a land where for four hundred years black blood has been shed unremarked and with impunity. America has never truly been outraged by the murder of a black man, woman, or child. White politicians may, if Negroes are aroused by a particular murder, say with their lips what they know with their minds they should feel with their hearts — but don't.

It is a measure of what the Negro feels that when the two white and one black civil rights workers were murdered in Mississippi in 1964, the event was welcomed by Negroes on a level of understanding beyond and deeper than the grief they felt for the victims and their families. This welcoming of violence and death to whites can almost be heard — indeed it can be heard — in the inevitable words, oft repeated by Negroes, that those whites, and blacks, do not die in vain. So it was with Mrs. Viola Liuzzo. And much of the anger which Negroes felt toward Martin Luther King during the Battle of Selma stemmed from the fact that he denied history a great moment, never to be recaptured, when he turned tail on the Edmund Pettus Bridge and refused to all those whites behind him what they had traveled thousands of miles to receive. If the police had turned them back by force, all those nuns, priests, rabbis, preachers, and distinguished ladies and gentlemen old and young — as they had done the Negroes a week earlier — the violence and brutality of the system would have been ruthlessly exposed. Or if, seeing King determined to lead them on to Montgomery, the troopers had stepped aside to avoid precisely the confrontation that Washington would not have tolerated, it would have signaled the capitulation of the militant white South. As it turned out, the March on Montgomery was a show of somewhat dim luster, stage-managed by the Establishment. But by this time the young whites were already active participants in the Negro revolution. In fact they had begun to transform it into something broader, with the potential of encompassing the whole of America in a radical re-ordering of society.

The fourth stage, now in its infancy, sees these white youth taking the initiative, using techniques learned in the Negro struggle to attack problems in the general society. The classic example of this new energy in action was the student battle on the UC campus at Berkeley, California — the Free Speech Movement. Leading the revolt were veterans of the civil rights movement, some of whom spent time on the firing line in the wilderness of Mississippi/ Alabama. Flowing from the same momentum were student demonstrations against U.S. interference in the internal affairs of Vietnam, Cuba, the Dominican Republic, and the Congo and U.S. aid to apartheid in South Africa. The students even aroused the intellectual community to actions and positions unthinkable a few years ago: witness the teach-ins. But their revolt is deeper than single-issue protest. The characteristics of the white rebels which most alarm their elders — the long hair, the new dances, their love for Negro music, their use of marijuana, their mystical attitude toward sex — are all tools of their rebellion. They have turned these tools against the totalitarian fabric of American society — and they mean to change it.

From the beginning America has been a schizophrenic nation. Its two conflicting images of itself were never reconciled, because never before has the survival of its most cherished myths made a reconciliation mandatory. Once before, during the bitter struggle between North and South climaxed by the Civil War, the two images of Amercia came into conflict, although whites North and South scarcely understood it. The image of America held by its most alienated citizens was advanced neither by the North nor by the South; it was perhaps best expressed by Frederick Douglass, who was born into slavery in 1817, escaped to the North, and became the greatest leader-spokesman for the blacks of his era. In words that can still, years later, arouse an audience of black Americans, Frederick Douglass delivered, in 1852, a scorching indictment in his Fourth of July oration in Rochester:

> What to the American slave is your Fourth of July? I answer: a day that reveals to him, more than all other days in the year, the gross injustic and cruelty to which he is the constant victim. To him your celebration is a sham; your boasted liberty, an unholy license; your national greatness, swelling vanity; your sounds of rejoicing are empty and heartless; your denunciation of tyrants, brass-fronted impudence; your shouts of liberty and equality, hollow mockery; your prayers and hymns, your sermons and thanksgivings, with all your religious parade and solemnity, are, to him, more bombast, fraud, deception, impiety and hypocrisy — a thin veil to cover up crimes which would disgrace a nation of savages. . . .
>
> You boast of your love of liberty, your superior civilization, and your pure Christianity, while the whole political power of the nation (as embodied in the two great political parties) is solemnly pledged to support and perpetuate the enslavement of three millions of your countrymen. You hurl your anathemas at the crown-headed tyrants of Russia and Austria and pride yourselves on your democratic institutions, while you yourselves consent to be the mere *tools* and *bodyguards* of the tyrants of Virginia and Carolina.
>
> You invite to your shores fugitives of oppression from abroad, honor them with banquets, greet them with ovations, cheer them, toast them, salute them, protect them, and pour out your money to

them like water; but the fugitive from your own land you advertise, hunt, arrest, and kill. You glory in your refinement and your universal education; yet you maintain a system as barbarous and dreadful as ever stained the character of a nation — a system begun in avarice, supported in pride, and perpetuated in cruelty.

You shed tears over fallen Hungary, and make the sad story of her wrongs the theme of your poets, statesmen and orators, till your gallant sons are ready to fly to arms to vindicate her cause against the oppressor; but, in regard to the ten thousand wrongs of the American slave, you would enforce the strictest silence, and would hail him as an enemy of the nation who dares to make these wrongs the subject of public discourse!

This most alienated view of America was preached by the Abolitionists, and by Harriet Beecher Stowe in her *Uncle Tom's Cabin*. But such a view of America was too distasteful to receive wide attention, and serious debate about America's image and her reality was engaged in only on the fringes of society. Even when confronted with overwhelming evidence to the contrary, most white Americans have found it possible, after steadying their rattled nerves, to settle comfortably back into their vaunted belief that America is dedicated to the proposition that all men are created equal and endowed by their Creator with certain inalienable rights — life, liberty and the pursuit of happiness. With the Constitution for a rudder and the Declaration of Independence as its guiding star, the ship of state is sailing always toward a brighter vision of freedom and justice for all.

Because there is no common ground between these two contradictory images of America, they had to be kept apart. But the moment the blacks were let into the white world — let out of the voiceless and faceless cages of their ghettos, singing, walking, talking, dancing, writing, and orating *their* image of America and of Americans — the white world was suddenly challenged to match its practice to its preachments. And this is why those whites who abandon the *white* image of America and adopt the *black* are greeted with such unmitigated hostility by their elders.

For all these years whites have been taught to believe in the myth they preached, while Negroes have had to face the bitter reality of what America practiced. But without the lies and distortions, white Americans would not have been able to do the things they have done. When whites are forced to look honestly upon the objective proof of their deeds, the cement of mendacity holding white society together swiftly disintegrates. On the other hand, the core of the black world's vision remains intact, and in fact begins to expand and spread into the psychological territory vacated by the non-viable white lies, i.e., into the minds of young whites. It is remarkable how the system worked for so many years, how the majority of whites remained effectively unaware of any contradiction between their view of the world and that world itself. The mechanism by which this was rendered possible requires examination at this point.

Let us recall that the white man, in order to justify slavery and, later on, to justify segregation, elaborated a complex, all-pervasive myth which at one time classified the black man as a subhuman beast of burden. The myth was progressively modified, gradually elevating the blacks on the scale of evolution, following their slowly changing status, until the plateau of separate-but-equal was reached at the close of the nineteenth century. During slavery, the black was seen as a mindless Supermasculine Menial. Forced to do the backbreaking work, he was conceived in terms of his ability to do such work — "field niggers," etc. The white man administered the plantation, doing all the thinking, exercising omnipotent power over the slaves. He had little difficulty dissociating himself from the black slaves, and he could not conceive of their positions being reversed or even reversible.

Blacks and whites being conceived as mutually exclusive types, those attributes imputed to the blacks could not also be imputed to the whites — at least not in equal degree — without blurring the line separating the races. These images were based upon the social function of the two races, the work they performed. The ideal white man was one who knew how to use his head, who knew how to manage and control things and get things done. Those whites who were not in a position to perform these functions nevertheless aspired to them. The ideal black man was one who did exactly as he was told, and did it efficiently and cheerfully. "Slaves," said Frederick Douglass, "are generally expected to sing as well as to work." As the black man's position and function became more varied, the images of white and black, having become stereotypes, lagged behind.

The separate-but-equal doctrine was promulgated by the Supreme Court in 1896. It had the same purpose domestically as the Open Door Policy toward China in the international arena: to stabilize a situation and subordinate a non-white population so that racist exploiters could manipulate those people according to their own selfish interests. These doctrines were foisted off as *the epitome of enlightened justice, the highest expression of morality.* Sanctified by religion, justified by philosophy and legalized by the Supreme Court, separate-but-equal was enforced by day by agencies of the law, and by the KKK & Co. under cover of night. Booker T. Washington, the Martin Luther King of his day, accepted separate-but-equal in the name of all Negroes. W. E. B. DuBois denounced it.

Separate-but-equal marked the last stage of the white man's flight into cultural neurosis, and the beginning of the black man's frantic striving to assert his humanity and equalize his position with the white. Blacks ventured into all fields of endeavor to which they could gain entrance. Their goal was to present in all fields a performance that would equal or surpass that of the whites. It was long axiomatic among blacks that a black had to be twice as competent as a white in any field in order to win grudging recognition from the whites. This produced a pathological motivation in the blacks to equal or surpass the whites, and a pathological motivation in the whites to maintain a distance from the blacks. This is the rack on which black and white Americans receive their delicious torture! At first there was the color bar, flatly denying the blacks entrance to certain spheres of activity. When this no longer worked, and blacks invaded sector after sector of American life and economy, the whites evolved other methods of keeping their distance. The illusion of the Negro's inferior nature had to be maintained.

One device evolved by the whites was to tab whatever the blacks did with the prefix "Negro." We had *Negro* literature, *Negro* athletes, *Negro* music, *Negro* doctors, *Negro* politicians, *Negro* workers. The malignant ingeniousness of this device is that although it accurately describes an objective biological fact — or, at least, a sociological fact in America — it concealed the paramount psychological fact: that to the white mind, prefixing anything with "Negro" automatically consigned it to an inferior category. A well-known example of the white necessity to deny due credit to blacks is in the realm of music. White musicians were famous for going to Harlem and other Negro cultural centers literally to steal the black man's music, carrying it back across the color line into the Great White World and passing off the watered-down loot as their own original creations. Blacks, meanwhile, were ridiculed as *Negro* musicians playing inferior coon music.

The Negro revolution at home and national liberation movements abroad have unceremoniously shattered the world of fantasy in which the whites have been living. It is painful that many do not yet see that their fantasy world has been rendered uninhabitable in the last half of the twentieth century. But it is away from this world that the white youth of today are turning. The "paper tiger" hero, James Bond, offering the whites a triumphant image of themselves, is saying what many whites want desperately to hear reaffirmed: *I am still the White Man, lord of the land, licensed to kill, and the world is still an empire at my feet.* James Bond feeds on that secret little anxiety, the psychological white backlash, felt in some degree by most whites alive. It is exasperating to see little brown men and little yellow men from the mysterious Orient, and the opaque black men of Africa (to say nothing of these impudent American Negroes!) who come to the UN and talk smart to us, who are scurrying all over *our* globe in their strange modes of dress — much as if they were new, unpleasant arrivals from another planet. Many whites believe in their ulcers that it is only a matter of time before the Marines get the signal to round up these truants and put them back securely in their cages. But it is away from this fantasy world that the white youth of today are turning.

In the world revolution now under way, the initiative rests with people of color. That growing numbers of white youth are repudiating their heritage of blood and taking people of color as their heroes and models is a tribute not only to their insight but to the resilience of the human spirit. For today the heroes of the initiative are people not usually thought of as white: Fidel Castro, Che Guevara, Kwame Nkrumah, Mao Tse-tung, Gamal Abdel Nasser, Robert F. Williams, Malcolm X, Ben Balla, John Lewis, Martin Luther King, Jr., Robert Parris Moses, Ho Chi Minh, Stokely Carmichael, W. E. B. DuBois, James Forman, Chou En-lai.

The white youth of today have begun to react to the fact that the "American Way of Life" is a fossil of history. What do they care if their old baldheaded and crew-cut elders don't dig their caveman mops? They couldn't care less about the old, stiffassed honkies who don't like their new dances: Frug, Monkey, Jerk, Swim, Watusi. All they know is that it feels good to swing to way-out body-rhythms instead of dragassing across the dance floor like zombies to the dead beat of mind-smothered Mickey Mouse music. Is it any wonder that the youth have lost all respect for their elders, for law and order, when for as long as they can remember all they've witnessed is a monumental bickering over the Negro's place in American society and the right of people around the world to be left alone by outside powers? They have witnessed the law, both domestic and international, being spat upon by those who do not like its terms. Is it any wonder, then, that they feel justified, by sitting-in and freedom riding, in breaking laws made by lawless men? Old funny-styled, zipper-mouthed political night riders know nothing but to haul out an investigating committee to *look into the disturbance* to find the cause of the unrest among the youth. Look into a mirror! The cause is you, Mr. and Mrs. Yesterday, you with your forked tongues.

A young white today cannot help but recoil from the base deeds of his people. On every side, on every continent, he sees racial arrogance, savage brutality toward the conquered and subjugated people, genocide; he sees the human cargo of the slave trade; he sees the systematic extermination of American Indians; he sees the civilized nations of Europe fighting in imperial depravity over the lands of other people — and over possession of the very people themselves. There seems to be no end to the ghastly deeds of which his people are guilty. *GUILTY*. The slaughter of the Jews by the Germans, the dropping of atomic bombs on the Japanese people — these deeds weigh heavily upon the prostrate souls and tumultuous consciences of the white youth. The white heroes, their hands dripping with blood, are dead.

The young whites know that the colored people of the world, Afro-Americans included, do not seek revenge for their suffering. They seek the same things the white rebel wants: an end to war and exploitation. Black and white, the young rebels are free people, free in a way that Americans have never been before in the history of their country. And they are outraged.

There is in America today a generation of white youth that is truly worthy of a black man's respect, and this is a rare event in the foul annals of American history. From the beginning of the contact between blacks and whites, there has been very little reason for a black man to respect a white, with such exceptions as John Brown and others lesser known. But respect commands itself and it can neither be given nor withheld when it is due. If a man like Malcolm X could change and repudiate racism, if I myself and other former Muslims can change, if young whites can change, then there is hope for America. It was certainly strange to find myself, while steeped in the doctrine that all whites were devils by nature, commanded by the heart to applaud and acknowledge respect for these young whites — despite the fact that they are descendants of the masters and I the descendant of slave. The sins of the fathers are visited upon the heads of the children — but only if the children continue in the evil deeds of the fathers.

A. Significant Collections of Essays by Individual Black Writers

Baldwin, James. *The Fire Next Time.* New York: Dial, 1963.

‾‾‾‾‾‾*Nobody Knows My Name.* New York: Dial, 1961.

‾‾‾‾‾‾*Notes of a Native Son.* Boston: Beacon, 1955.

Bennett, Lerone, Jr. *The Negro Mood.* Chicago: Johnson, 1965.

Brown, William Wells. *The Black Man: His Antecedents, His Genius, and His Achievements.* New York: Thomas Hamilton; Boston: Wallcut, 1863.

Cleaver, Eldridge. *Soul on Ice.* New York: McGraw-Hill, 1968.

DuBois, W. E. B. *The Souls of Black Folk: Essays and Sketches.* Chicago: McClurg, 1903; Blue Heron, 1953.

Ellison, Ralph. *Shadow and Act.* New York: Random House, 1964.

Hernton, Calvin C. *White Papers for White Americans.* Garden City, New York: Doubleday, 1967.

Jones, LeRoi. *Home: Social Essays.* New York: Morrow, 1966.

Killens, John O. *Black Man's Burden.* New York: Trident, 1965.

King, Martin Luther, Jr. *Why We Can't Wait.* New York: Harper, 1964.

Miller, Kelly. *An Appeal to Conscience.* New York: Macmillan, 1918.

‾‾‾‾‾‾*The Everlasting Stain.* Washington: Associated Publishers, 1924.

‾‾‾‾‾‾*Out of the House of Bondage.* New York: Crowell, 1914.

‾‾‾‾‾‾*Race Adjustment; Essays on the Negro in America.* New York: Schocken, 1968. (Originally pub. by Neale, 1908.)

Redding, Saunders. *On Being Negro in America.* Indianapolis: Bobbs-Merrill, 1951.

Williams, John A. *This Is My Country Too.* New York: New American Library, 1965.

Wright, Richard. *White Man; Listen!* New York: Doubleday, 1957.

B. Other Anthologies Including Essays by Black Writers

The American Negro Writer and His Roots. New York: American Society of African Culture, 1960.

Brown, Sterling A., Arthur P. Davis, and Ulysses Lee, eds. *The Negro Caravan*. New York: Dryden, 1941.

Calverton, Victor F., ed. *An Anthology of American Negro Literature*. New York: Modern Library, 1929.

Chapman, Abraham, ed. *Black Voices*. New York: Dell, 1968.

Cromwell, Otelia; Lorenzo D. Turner, and Eva B. Dykes, eds. *Readings from Negro Authors*. New York: Harcourt, Brace, 1931.

Culp, Daniel, ed. *Twentieth Century Negro Literature or a Cyclopedia of Thought*. Naperville, Illinois: Nichols, 1902.

Dreer, Herman. *American Literature by Negro Authors*. New York: Macmillan, 1950.

Ebony Magazine Editors, eds. *The White Problem in America*. Chicago: Johnson, 1967.

Hill, Herbert. *Soon, One Morning: New Writings by American Negroes, 1940–1962*. New York: Knopf, 1963.

Locke, Alain, ed. *The New Negro; an Interpretation*. New York: Boni, 1925.

Turner, Darwin T., and Jean M. Bright, eds. *Images of the Negro in America*. Boston: Heath, 1965.

Watkins, Sylvester C., ed. *Anthology of American Negro Literature*. New York: Modern Library, 1944.

Williams, John A., ed. *The Angry Black*. New York: Lancer, 1962.

_____*Beyond the Angry Black*. New York: Cooper Square, 1966.